I0141645

# ON COMMON GROUND

by
Sharon Kahrar

# On Common Ground

# ON COMMON GROUND
by
Sharon Kahrar

All rights reserved. This book, or parts thereof,
may not be reproduced
in any form without written permission
from the publisher.

Copyright © September 22, 2014
Sharon Kahrar
All rights reserved

ISBN-13: 978-0989802932  — paperback
ISBN: 1484933516  — e-book

Second Edition

Website: http://sharonkahrar24.net

Published by Visions of Reality
PO Box 128
Chalfont, PA  18914
215-996-0646

Printed in the United States of America

# DEDICATION

*For you, dear reader, who desire*
*to follow your intuition,*
*while deepening your connection to Spirit.*

# CONTENTS

## ACKNOWLEDGEMENTS

I deeply appreciate my youngest son, James Kahrar, as he was the first to encourage me to write and journal my God experiences. Additionally, I would like to thank my family; husband Bernie, oldest son Bryan, and daughter Jocelynn, for their support. I am ever grateful for my sister, Bonnie Cullum for her constant support and comfort as we travel together this fragile road of life. Finally, I would like to thank my Spiritual Teacher, Elizabeth Joyce, who helped me deepen and recognize how Spirit always walks with us on our journey.

# FOREWORD

*On Common Ground* is a wonderful true-life story of a woman's quest for her personal Spiritual enlightenment. It is a remarkable fusion of wisdom and practicality that emerges from a deep Spiritual love and sense of purpose. This book, coming together from the author's journaling over decades, brings the reader inspiration, while Sharon is clearing away the obstacles to creating love and compassion in her life. So many of these stories are very human, as the author struggles within herself to understand life's circumstances. Sharon shows us how to bring these Spiritual techniques into our life, quickly and easily, reminding us all the while that everything happens for a reason.

This is a timely book, as we are well into the second decade of the Twenty-first Century. Many of us are seeking some kind of Spiritual relief and inner peace from all of the changes we are facing, physical, emotional, and practical, and the decisions that must be addressed in our lives. Sharon Kahrar shows us that once we solve the mystery of our ego blockages and find this wonderful, unconditional love dwelling deep inside, we will begin to see *and know* that love is everywhere. Sharon carefully reminds us that it's not enough to know all these things, but we must be prepared to take action ourselves to walk our personal destiny.

Elizabeth Joyce
Chalfont, PA
March 26, 2013

Website: www.new-visions.com

xii

# ON COMMON GROUND

# PREFACE

I've always known there's a book within me to be written about what I've experienced and learned. It is my intention that those who choose to read *On Common Ground* find it an easy read as if speaking with close friends. This book is not geared toward those content with their Spiritual beliefs but rather aimed at the seeker who, like myself, searches for truth with Spirit, and a deeper connection. In this writing I will share many of my personal experiences and some of the questions I was compelled to ask God in my meager attempts to understand this 'energetic connection' that unites all of us.

When my Spiritual journey kicked into high gear, my experiences seem different from those of the general public; at least they are not openly discussed. This adventure is written with the hope that those who experience things out of the ordinary, such as your 6th Sense, will benefit; or at the very least, take comfort in knowing they are not alone.

In late winter of 2000, my husband Bernie and I chose to vacation in Southern Spain. We met two women; Linda, widowed less than a year and her friend, Terry. They were long time friends, and Terry hoped this vacation would lift Linda's Spirit after her devastating loss. The four of us hit it off from the get-go, and during the week we enjoyed several outings and meals together.

One evening Linda opened up to me and shared the story of her husband's recent passing and how it impacted their family. This led us into a deeper discussion on prayer and religion. Suddenly Terry interjects that she doesn't agree with what I'm saying. As I turned to her, touching her arm, I said, "It's really okay, we can disagree, there is no right or wrong here. With so many people in this world, there are many different ways to get to God." We discussed a few other things before parting for the evening.

During the night I awoke and, while restless, I began to pray by thanking God I had met these wonderful women; I asked that God bless Linda and her family as they go through the grief process, and then I asked God to bless Terry, who is so passionate about her beliefs. I continued with, "I am so grateful Terry and I can travel such different paths, yet come to stand before You on common ground." An inner voice interrupted my reverie saying, "The name of the book!" I thought, "Huh? The name of what book?" Then I realized, "Oh, *On Common Ground* is the name of my book to be written…Wow!"

NOTES:

On Common Ground

NOTES:

# CHAPTER 1
## 1950 –1970's

## QUESTIONS

The beginning is always the best place to start, so I must travel back to my childhood, at around five years old. One night I had something happen I will never forget. My bedroom was in the rear of our row house on Taylor Avenue in Baltimore, MD, next to my parent's room. From the window in my room, you could see our back yard and the alley leading out to the street. Back then our street lamps had tin shades and were always on at night, so my bedroom was never totally dark. I woke up in the middle of the night and there was a shadow standing at the foot of my bed. It was the color of black ink in the shape of a man, and there was a yellow-green sparkling light that outlined his shape. Although I was very young, I thought to myself, "I'm dreaming," while rubbing my eyes. When I opened them again it was still standing there … a black form, so solid that part of my chest of drawers was blocked. I quickly pulled the covers over my head and called for my mother, who gave me a baby aspirin to calm me down after my so-called "bad dream" and helped me go back to sleep.

This experience came to my mind again when I was a teenager, and saw iridescent pink nail polish on my mother's nails for the first time. I thought, "Oh," to myself as I remembered the sparking yellow-green light. This left me wondering about that prior experience all over again.

Fast forward to the year 1983, I am 32, married and living in New Jersey. My neighbors asked me to go to a free lecture at the local high school, and as the mother of three, I jumped at the chance to have an evening out. The lecture was given by a group from Silva Mind Control, and was so interesting. I am not sure of his name, but I do remember that this seminar was given by a former priest, who shared his story with us. A large movie screen was pulled down behind him because we would be viewing a series of slides. I was very relaxed and captivated by his presentation, when I noticed a sparkling yellow-green light around the outline of his body. I realized I was seeing this light because I thought to myself, there must be stage lights shining on him for this to happen, and promptly returned my attention to his riveting story. After the intermission, the priest mentioned that several people asked him about a yellow-green light running around the outline of his body – he said this was his "Aura." I sat there in shock realizing I was able to see something only a few people there had seen. It wasn't until days later, when I'm home, that I realized this wasn't the first time I had seen this shimmering light—but now, the black ink shape has been filled by the shape of the priest. Does this mean I should join Silva Mind Control? At the time, that would have been a luxury for me and would have taxed our family budget, so I stored the incident in the same corner of my mind where I put the dream. Periodically I wondered if my "experience and his aura" were related, and what it all meant.

I am not a *special* child who knows or sees things on a Spiritual level; my youth was filled with love and an abundance of free time—to just grow up. One time in Baltimore, when I was very young, I got up during the night to go into the bathroom to get a drink, and while I was walking, a thought popped into my head, "Turn on the light, there might be a spider in the cup on the sink." I turned on the light and when I looked into the cup, there indeed was a spider! Our family moved to Aberdeen, MD in 1957; I was eleven. A few years later, mother joined the Bible Baptist Church. There were a lot of good things that happened to me, but my strongest memories are of two incidents that caused me to experience great fear.

One Sunday, the passionate pastor was up at the pulpit giving a heart-felt plea for people to come forward to be saved. He was winding down his sermon when he said, "I believe God tries to get you for only so long … then God stops!" … WHAT? God stop trying, for me? That was horrifying for this teenager, and as I sat there in the pew, with my heart pounding out of my chest, I was deeply frightened! This pastor instilled a deep fear in me that lasted for many years.

When I was about fifteen, on another memorable Sunday, our passionate pastor is again pleading for those who need to be saved to come forward. This pastor even had us feeling sorry for the Baptist Church down the road, because that church was called Baptist "Bible" Church. We were called the "Bible" Baptist Church, and their belief wasn't as Bible-based as ours. Watching this man's passionate plea, I asked a question I have never forgotten, *"God, is this all a head game?"* Stunned, that at fifteen years of age I would pose such a question to the God I knew, along with the fear and nausea that instantly gripped my stomach, made this another memorable moment.

I don't know whether it was lack of faith, or Spiritual/religious immaturity, but in my twenties, I was very angry with God. No, that's not quite right. I did have faith by the very fact I was angry with the "big guy," it stands to reason I *knew* that God existed.

I had two issues with God. First, what kind of a God would wait so long to send his Son, Jesus, to save us all? How about all the other people who had lived before? Did they count for nothing? Secondly, I always considered God around the corner; never close by, as if I were separated from Him. If I was especially *good*, God cared, or, if I was especially *bad*, God cared, but on a daily basis God was not concerned with me. This concept of mine was about to radically change as I was taught that God was closer than my nearest breath.

NOTES:

NOTES:

## Chapter II

## 1980's

**THE VOICES BEGIN**

Between ages thirty-seven to forty-three, I heard three distinct voices; the voices, or Divine messages, have happened many times since, but these voices were the first. The first time was when a neighbor at our summer place died suddenly. My husband was at our summer get-a-way with our three young children and he called to tell me what had happened to Joe.  I was upset and wondered how I would be able to drive up to North Jersey during rush hour to attend his wake.

Unhealthy patterns from my youth were still in effect for me when we met this fine couple, Joe and Barbara, many years before at our summer get-a-way. They

11

heard me introduced as Sheryl. Joe corrected himself after a year when he asked me what my name really was. I thought it was cute they called me Sheryl. I greatly admired this couple. Joe had many health issues including blindness, but they had a strong relationship that I envied because my husband and I put our children, work, education, car, house, etc., etc. ahead of developing a closer bond.

Upon arriving at the funeral parlor I walked up to his wife Barbara. I was so upset I didn't see the receiving line that wrapped halfway around the parlor until I was on my way out! His kind wife turned to console me. Then I turned from her towards Joe's casket. For the first time in my life, instead of saying a memorized prayer, I talked to Joe as if he could hear me. I told him I really liked him and was so sorry that this had happened. Then I mentally said something that surprised even me. *"Well Joe, now you know what I look like."* I wished him God-speed, said Amen, and left after signing the visitor's book. In the parking lot, I was sitting alone in my car, face in hands, tears streaming, nose totally clogged, talking to God. "Oh God, what's going to happen to her, they were so close; poor Barbara. Oh God, what will she do— what will she do?" In the middle of my agony, a strong voice interrupted my sobbing, "She'll be alright, Sheryl!" Shocked, my hands dropped away and even though I was aware this voice was in my head, my eyes turned to the right,– no cars; to the left – only an empty car, and my windows were rolled up. I was acutely aware I'd heard this voice smack-dab in the middle of my head, years later realizing it had been a telepathic way of communicating. I had no doubt it was the voice of my friend Joe, that I had minutes before prayed over. So, I answered him, "Okay, Joe."

For years, I wondered *why* Joe was there and *why* he spoke to me. I became very emotional whenever I recalled this experience, and it never failed to make me cry. This shook my religious foundation to the core and I couldn't think of anyone to ask about this kind of experience that wouldn't think I would need extensive therapy.

I began searching. My protestant background said, *"Death is a sleep like state."* My years attending a Catholic Church told me when we die we are judged before we look on the face of God; others go to purgatory and hopefully work their way out, and some even feel there is nothing after this life. Okay fine, this still didn't explain why my friend spoke to me in my car.

The second inner voice happened three years later at forty in a small, two-seater beauty parlor in Passaic, NJ. I was waiting for the young woman to wash my hair, when she remarked to the three of us waiting that she had a horrible headache, so bad she was feeling "sick to her stomach." The two other women gave advice. One said, "Smoke a cigarette," the other, "Eat a bagel; it will constrict the vessels and bring the blood down to the stomach."

I was mindlessly flipping through the pages in a magazine, when casually I started a telepathic dialogue with God about the nice lady with the headache, "Oh God, I know how it feels to have a headache like that." A voice within interrupted me saying, "Go help her." My initial response was, "No! I'd be embarrassed!" Instantly, I reassessed my situation and said to myself, "Sharon, you stupid ass, something just told you to go help her and you said no." No doubt I failed the course in Bravery 101!

Finally realizing I was not doing this alone, I walked over to her and said, "I know a trick that might help you." I told the young woman with the headache this was something my husband does and it has always relieved my sick headaches. I asked her to sit in a chair, relax, and breathe deeply while I began to massage her neck and shoulders. "Recently," I said, "On the cover of the *Sunday Parade Magazine* section, there were nurses featured from Columbia Hospital in New York City." These nurses were the first to begin a program called *Therapeutic Touch*. The article said, *If someone with a broken arm came into the hospital, one of these nurses would hold her hand over their break – and it would take the pain away for up to four hours.* As I calmed this young woman with the headache, I applied pressure on certain key spots around her head, (Pressure points). When finished I said I hoped she felt better, and went back to my chair to wait for my wash and haircut.

I forgot all about this young woman, and as I was putting on my coat to leave, one of the concerned women asked her how her headache was, and she said, "Much better." The first woman said, "I told you to smoke a cigarette!" The other, "I told you to eat a bagel," but the young woman, pointing to me said, "No, what she did helped." Just ten years later I would say something quite different, but what I said at the time was, "See, I'm better than aspirin," as I took all the glory! That is what is called an EGO response!

The voices unnerved me and I made a visit to the library and took out a very thick book on schizophrenia. I am not educated medically and this book was not an easy one to understand, but I gleaned from the people's stories that the voices I read about in this book were not what I was experiencing.

I went to see a numerologist in Maryland, and I told her about the voices I was hearing. This woman had been a nun, and she told me she thought I was a natural mystic. Being raised Protestant, I had no idea what that was, so when I returned to New Jersey, I looked it up in the dictionary. Once I began reading books on mystical and saintly experiences, I was comforted because the books described these Spiritual voices to be more in line with what I was experiencing.

The third inner voice occurred three years later. Over the years I watched two segments of Sixty Minutes about betrothed women in India who, when rejected or disgraced, either set themselves on fire, or a member of their family would do the dastardly deed. I was horrified by this tradition and since it still continued, according to the follow-up program years later, there were twenty-five percent less woman in India than in the general population around our world. From then on deep resentment would swell inside of me every time I saw a man from India. Over time I realized this negative thinking would hurt me far more than it would ever hurt anyone in India, especially when I came across a saying, *"acid corrodes the vessel as well as what you put it on."* I admit, far too often I would partake in jokes about how "they" drive, or how "their" clothes smelled like their spices. I am sure everyone knows someone who behaved like I did. I had become deeply prejudiced. Growing up, my immediate family was blessed because we had a mother who did not harbor prejudice for any race and I knew instinctively this feeling inside was not good for me. Our daughter, Jocelynn, a teenager at the time, heard me talking and said, "Ma, I can't believe this is you. You never talk about anyone like that!" This comment of hers was right on the mark and only left me feeling worse.

One day on my way home after work, I experienced the third voice. I coasted slowly to a stop at a red light and in front - on the passenger side of my car, stood a woman from India, exquisitely dressed from head to toe in her full sari. Relaxed and leaning on my console, I gazed up at her. I mused, "Oh ... beautiful, Lord, beautiful," when a voice interrupted my reverie with, "She is your sister!" I quickly bolted upright, feeling instant nausea and headache all in one shot! I drove home and told my husband I had experienced another voice.

This voice posed a huge problem for me because I had one sister; she is five years younger than me. All the women in this world are okay and I have really great girlfriends, *but I have only one sister!* (These old patterns of thinking were very difficult for me to give up.) This voice spiraled me into days of inner reflection, and I eventually concluded that, if this woman from India was my "sister," that meant that men from India were my "brothers." My first thought was "Yuk!" I needed to reaffirm constantly to myself there had been another inner voice message.

I wish this voice would say more than one sentence. Who is this that interrupts when I am deep in thought causing me to question and readjust my life, along with my core beliefs? Wherever this voice comes from, I knew once again things were about to change and I would never be the same. The *personal decisions* I resolved to make were:

> 1) To stop participating in sarcasm directed at any race, or anyone else for any reason.

> 2) Whenever I saw a man or woman from India (whether happy, sad, sick, rich or poor), I asked God to be with them. I would send many prayer bubbles upward on my way to and from work. Consequently, it took time, but I learned it's hard to feel resentment for anyone when you pray for them.

Many years later, I read that to hear the type of voices I hear is called "Spiritual clairaudience." I'm not crazy! It has a name! Oh Lord, it has a name!

## YEEE-OUCH!

One fall evening during 1986, our 15-year-old son, Bryan, and his father were downstairs in the family room. I was upstairs kneeling underneath the dining room table, dusting and polishing the table legs. They began to argue and I was getting upset because I could tell this was going to escalate. I knew that shortly I would need to go downstairs; separate and defuse this argument, or it would get out of hand.

I start agonizing to God, "What about Bryan? What are we going to do with Bryan? Dear God, what is going to happen to Bryan?" In the next instant, I felt a hand reach through the table and firmly take hold of my right shoulder. A strong voice spoke, "Bryan will be all right." A feeling like cool water began at the top of my head, sliding down my upper body. Although it seems funny now, I think I did what anyone else would have done; I hit my head trying to get out from under the table!

When standing, I thanked God for these comforting words. I guess one gets used to these Divine interruptions over time. Once downstairs, I separated the two of them, putting an end to their argument. Bryan ran out of the room and up to his bedroom. I informed my husband Bernie, "I've heard another voice."

These simple words would occasionally pop into my mind and they sustained me throughout Bryan's teenage years. *"Bryan will be all right!"* Today Bryan is much more than all right as a father as well as a successful businessman.

## PRACTICAL APPLICATION

Over the years talking to God, *whatever God is,* intensified for me. Always, when I wake up in the morning,

I begin the day being grateful, continuing the blessings in the shower, on the way to work, at lunch, on the way home from work, and before I go to sleep. If I happen to wake in the middle of the night, the gratitude continues. Was it possible for God to get tired of hearing from me? It seemed I was doing an enormous amount of talking, contemplation, and inner reflection; there eventually came a time when I felt I was not being heard; please remember, at this point, I was doing *all* the talking! I think it is natural for people, at some point, to ask for a sign from God. This is one way I hoped to prove to myself that what one can't see does in fact exist.

One day, when driving to work, I was praying when, all of a sudden, I thought, "You know what, God? I talk to you all the time, but it feels like there is a brick wall in front of my face, and that you are not hearing me! I am going to be like Jason and the Argonauts; I am throwing out a golden fleece! If you choose, pick it up, and then let me know if You hear me. Amen." My passing thought was I *must* have passed Bravery 101.

A week or so later, I arrived at our new office at work and the Sales Manger told me that his father was going to have an operation that day. I am not a nut about it, but throughout the day, whenever the Sales Manager passed by me, I sent up several *positive thought bubbles.* I was asking God to watch over this man's father, to guide the surgeon's hand, gratitude for the nurses that gave such good care, the anesthesiologist, and to please hold the entire family in His comforting hand, etc." Bubble by bubble.

Near the end of the day, the Sales Manager was about twenty feet from my desk searching for something in the files. The phone rang and when I answered, it's for him. As I turned to alert him, my mouth felt full of rocks, and my tongue stumbled over itself, and I had trouble articulating and what comes out was, "…ub-blub-blub, er, Frank, you have a call." Embarrassed, I quickly apologized and said, "I don't know why I called you Frank, I don't even know one right now." The Sales Manager walked toward me, holding his folded arms in front of his chest, and said to me, "I can't believe you have just called me my father's name." My head started to buzz, as I realized that although I may have forgotten my "You are not hearing me" challenge, obviously God hadn't!! On this day, from my very own mouth, dropped the name of a man I had never met, but had been sending positive healing prayer bubbles up for.

It seems God appreciates a challenge; at the very least, God, whatever God is, accepted mine. He probably figured, after hearing what must be gazillions of memorized, mechanical prayers, "Hey, there's a live one down there! Sharon is waking up!"

## THE SEARCH

I searched everywhere and the search became my deepest passion. I read good books and some strange ones. Oh my gosh what is strange anyway? What was happening to me surely wasn't normal. What's a girl to do and was there anyone out there who would talk about these things? The pattern seems to be; first I have an experience, then I am off in search of "what was that, why is it happening to me, and what does it all mean?" Somewhere in the back of my mind I thought, these are things I should be experiencing in church, but it seems God is bringing me through the back door to broaden my view of exactly what *God* is.

One of the books I learned so much from is called *The Writings of Florence Scovil Shinn*. These writings are a collection of four books that deal with affirmations and how they change your life. At the time, because of my Christian heritage, her books were comforting because she quoted text from the Bible. I was advised to read this collection of books by a Shiatsu massage master who gave me my first affirmation, taken from Shinn's book. This affirmation was: *"Endless kindness comes to me in endless ways, I deserve it and I accept it now."* I wrote this affirmation on yellow stickers and placed them by my phones at home and work, on my car visor, kitchen cabinets, bathroom mirrors, etc.

I thought of myself as a giving person, but definitely found it difficult to receive graciously. Really, they are only opposite sides of the same coin, but I couldn't stand feeling that I was bothering anyone if I asked for something. Endless kindness didn't seem too threatening, so I repeated this affirmation silently whenever I thought about it, and out loud, with enthusiasm, whenever I was alone. Several weeks passed before I received my first lesson in positive thinking and how it could change ones life!

One day I found a large glass in the kitchenette where I worked. I was happy because I was making an effort to drink more water. I used this glass several weeks when one Friday my good friend Eileen walked by my desk and said, "Sharon, YOU have MY glass!" I apologized, telling her I didn't know it was hers, and promised to clean and return it promptly to the kitchenette. I naturally began my inner dialogue, "Well Lord, now I need a glass, but it needs to be a large one because I want to drink more water." Imagine my shock and surprise Monday morning at work, when one of our salesmen came through the door, plunked a large, plastic, orange advertising mug down on my desk and said, "Don't ask me why, but my wife said you need this!" My insides were fluttering, but I could only muster a quiet "*thank you,*" because I was filled to the brim with amazement!

That same week I was opening the morning mail and there was a pair of sunglasses, advertising a mid-western company. I was choosing to live a truthful existence – my relationship with the company I worked for was strong and for me, the end no longer justified the means; just because I worked for a company doesn't entitle me to their scotch tape or pens. I "asked" my boss if I could have the sunglasses to keep in my new car. He graciously granted my request and I sent up another *bubble* request. "Now I need a sunglass case Lord, or they'll get scratched in the glove compartment." That very evening, I pulled into a parking space, opened my door, and on the ground was an empty cloth sunglass case. Hey, I like this endless kindness stuff!

I have spent a mid-sized fortune reading and studying so many books. I knew my foundational belief system was changing, big time! I promised God I'd never talk about my changing beliefs to our three children. They had been raised in the Catholic Church and I didn't want to confuse them. No longer shy, I press on that, "God, if You want them to know, please send them to me when they are ready, and I will do my best to answer all their questions."

The new, firmly established belief for me was that more often than not, we confuse organized religions with God. Religions are great for establishing social order, but have more in common with large corporations. Churches need God; God does not need churches! God is much more far-reaching than any corporation. Each person is nothing more than a pathway to God.

All too soon, the spring day arrives when our youngest son, James, then fourteen, said to me, "Ma, what is all this?" as he stood there, arms out, surveying my dining room table brimming with books on religions,

Bibles, dreams, numerology, alternative methods of healing, prayer, meditation, affirmations, philosophy, theology etc., etc., etc. My thought, "Oh God, you sent my youngest?" James and I began a discussion that day that has never ended.

One Sunday that fall of 1989, I was upstairs reading in bed, when James came in pacing back and forth at the end of my bed and said that he thinks he is going crazy. I looked over my granny-glasses at him and asked exactly what makes him think that? He told me, "If he doesn't see his friends home, he thinks something bad will happen to them or if he doesn't know his father and me are home in bed, he thinks we will die." I looked at him and told him, "You're right, you are going to go crazy thinking these kinds of thoughts."

I got off our old four-poster bed, propped up the pillows on the other side, told James to lie down on the bed because I had recently watched *Mind, Medicine and Miracles*, by Bernie Siegel, and thought this video might help him. I put it in the VCR and we both watched. I kept pausing because James kept asking questions, so I gave him control of the remote.

We discussed how to help his mind. After forty-five minutes or so, I could see James was very relaxed when suddenly he said, "Whoa Ma! Something just lifted off of me! I'm going downstairs!" As he got up to leave, I handed him a paperback copy of *The Power of Your Subconscious Mind*, by Joseph Murphy, telling him it's an interesting, quick read.

Later that winter, I was home on Sunday working with *The Phoenix Cards*, by Susan Sheppard and Toni Taylor, I had just purchased, similar to other divination decks. James came home, and I asked him to pick one of the cards he liked best. I started reading to him the message it gave, when he said, "Ma, know why I picked that card?

See the White Light around St. Peter on the card? That is like the White Light I saw in your room that afternoon I asked questions!"

I responded, "I experienced this White Light in a church."

I believe that the White Light some of us see is truly a spiritual healing source, used in hands on healing; example, chi, shakti, or reiki healing energy. It is a live energetic, active, vibration as well as healing and calming, that brings us knowledge and peace.

James said, "You can have it in a church?"

I replied, "You can have it in my bedroom?" Suddenly I was aware that White Light is everywhere, and can be accessed at any time, when needed. That experience changed his life. I am ever grateful to have played a small part in his spiritual awakening.

## A DREAM LIKE NO OTHER...AND MY GURU?

In the late 1980's, I attended metaphysical classes offered by the adult education program in the town where I lived. I found them fascinating and learned much new information. I incorporated all types of lectures and classes from 1985-1995, while faithfully studying the Bible. Near the end of the 1980s I experienced a powerful dream:

In this dream I was in a hotel walking from room to room, looking in each room, and shaking my head in sadness. Finally, I entered one of the rooms. There was a twin bed to my left and a woman with long dark hair, standing in the corner by the foot of the bed, staring intently at me. I didn't know who she was, but I *knew* she was a friend. The woman was scrunched into the corner of the room. In front of me was a fireplace with a picture over it, and to my right was a closet door. I looked at the woman and I said, "It's so sad, it's just so sad." Looking at the picture over the fireplace, I inhaled a large breath, pursed my lips, and blew the breath out slowly while moving my head from side to side. The air I exhaled looked like exhaust coming out of a truck–dissipating black smoke!

I looked at the woman saying, "What was that?" I inhaled a second deep breath and again the same thing happened, dissipating black smoke! I looked at her and said, "That's strange!" Then I turned to walk towards her, and instantaneously she was lying across the foot of the bed. I was standing over her with my right hand on her heart, and there were lightening bolts (or electricity) going from her eyes to mine and back to hers again. This was extremely startling! It woke me up, *but the electricity kept on flashing!*

Suddenly awakened, lying there in my old four-poster bed next to my husband, the electricity was still coursing all over the skin of my body! Good God, what could this be?

This is another "dream" I will never forget because my eyes were open as I felt the electricity coursing over my skin. I always wondered about it, instinctively knowing this was a "huge" experience! Actually, I had no clue at the time, but I was to learn my *kundalini* was activated. Just who was this woman, and why was I infused with such a forceful White Light?

In less than a year, synchronicity came into play, or what is now call *spontaneous healing.* I was led to a woman I lovingly call my Guru ('learned one or teacher,' thank you Webster's Dictionary). Visiting a metaphysical bookstore I checked out one of the items for sale. I chose a lecture cassette called *Practical Spirituality*, by Elizabeth Joyce. After listening to this lecture, I said to myself, "She was good! Just where is she from?" I turned the cassette over, and low and behold, read that she's from a town not thirty minutes from me. I called, made an appointment, and Elizabeth Joyce faxed me directions to her home, along with a copy of her *Psychics, Fact, Fraud, or Fiction,* that was featured in the November 1986 issue of *Woman's Day Magazine.* Holy hat! I well remember this article because I had kept the magazine a long time on my dining room table.

I joined her women's group and Elizabeth taught me the deepest forms of meditation and how to work with energy. After meeting Ammachi, the Hugging Saint from Kerala, India, Elizabeth released me in 1994, knowing I had reached a level of spiritual discipline and had absorbed all of her teachings. She was assured that I would continue with my spiritual practice, and I have to this day. I continue to listen and experience inwardly what the angels and inner guides provide for me.

As a cautionary word, I must tell you that I had to work through my *ego* because my question to myself was, "Am I one of God's chosen?" As far as I could discern, not everyone had these experiences." It was always my belief that God picked his own – you know, like Moses, Isaac, King David, or Jesus, his disciples, along with my understanding that it was God who chose the Saints.

It was at this point, another remnant of my Christian heritage melted away, because I no longer confused Jesus with God. Now, I deeply believe we make the conscious decision to start this God-relationship. We open the door! Have you ever seen the picture of Jesus holding a lantern and leaning his head towards an old door while knocking? The door has no handle; in other words, "God does not violate and has to be invited in." Shoot, I don't remember opening any door or extending an invitation, so why were these experiences happening to me? Could it have something to do with my constant dialogue with God?

I can tell you, *I ain't no saint*! I also don't like confusing explanations so, after much reflection, here is what happened to me. Using a scale of "0% to 100%" for thought forms with zero being extremely negative thought forms and one hundred percent being the most positive thought forms one can attain, I began my morning reflections with Norman Vincent Peals's book, *The Power of Positive Thinking*. As I matured, the negative/unhealthy thought patterns I held for so long no longer served me, and I began to make conscious decisions to live more on the positive side of thoughts and decisions. God doesn't want us to be saints; literally, if we improve ourselves, God, the Universal Force, energy or whatever you call this life force, can then step in and begin to change our life. It takes only the smallest amount, one step from us, and instantaneous responses from the Universe.

I have an aunt that told a story about her first husband. This handsome couple oozed sex appeal, but after years together, and three children, one day they were out riding in their car, my uncle was driving and my aunt was on the passenger side. She commented to him, "You know hon, we used to be so close, we'd sit together, hold hands and you'd put your arm around me … what happened to us?" With his hands on the wheel, he looked over at her and said, "Well, I didn't move." I use this as an analogy for God. We turn from God—God never turns from us! Thank God, that the fears my old pastor awakened in me are now erased forever! I think many religions have instilled way too much fear and guilt into their members by constantly waving the heaven or hell carrot in front of their noses. They always emphasize a loving heart, but during my Bible study days, I found the Bible speaks just as much about the mind as it does the heart. A heart is a pump for blood–that's it, period! The mind is the builder and needs to be trained to think differently.

For almost three years, I attended Elizabeth Joyce's weekly women's group and at one of the meetings I'm listening to a woman who attends as regularly as I do. She says, "You know, I have peace in my heart except for one thing – I hate Puerto Ricans. All I ask is that God heals my heart and removes this hate." Knowing that her "hate" is really coming from her mind, I said to her, "It's not your heart that needs to be healed, it's your mind! Change your thoughts and your heart will follow suit." *"Where there is anger, hatred or resentment in the mind, it creates a spot in the brain that God (or peace) is not able to penetrate."* (Course in Miracles) When the Christian religion encourages us to have the mind of Christ, it means we need to shepherd/monitor our thoughts and change our way of "THINKING."

## POSSESSION (Entities/Addictions)

I didn't understand possession and was always horrified by the movie, *The Exorcist*, which I never saw. It really unnerved me to think that God would allow this possession thing to happen–especially to children! I've learned the vices religions have warned us about are all fun –at first! We experience a high, a numbing sensation, or a sense of power from whichever vice we are attracted to; then we go on to choose whether or not to make it a part of our life. We can always count on the fact that our chosen vices will consume us along with all our energy. Despite this fact, when we have experienced those first euphoric feelings of excitement, daring, numbness, satisfaction or power, we invite it in anyway and end up beseeching God, "Why did *You* allow this to happen to me?"

**I love this American Indian fable:**

An old Indian woman is out in a field gathering wood for winter when she comes across a frozen brightly colored snake. She thinks, "it's so beautiful," and takes it back to her tee-pee, places it near the fireplace, covers it with a blanket, brings it food and begins rubbing the snake to warm it up. As the snake comes around, she continues admiring its beauty when suddenly; the snake reaches back and bites her. Shocked, she exclaims, "How could you bite me? I took you in when you were frozen, covered you, fed you, rubbed you until you were warm." The snake stared at her and hissed, "You knew I was a snake when you brought me in."

We are always in on the decision of what possesses us.

NOTES:

NOTES:

# Chapter III

## The 1990's

### WE HELP ORCHESTRATE HOW IT GOES DOWN

I took to heart this Universal Law about "what you think-happens." At first, this concept is a little more than unsettling to chew on; that I am somehow responsible for everything that happens in my life. Huh?? It was so much easier to blame God! After all God knows why the events in my life need to happen, *don't I deserve them?* Learning about this *what-you-think-happens* thing, kind of lets God off of the hot seat and puts me on it! Seems like it has more in common with Self-responsibility!

Louise Hay teaches, *"Thoughts are things."* Each thought has an electrical impulse. It can be measured, thrown out into the ethers, and boomerangs back to bite or kiss you! We are constantly creating our own lives by our thoughts. The clearest way I can explain this is to tell you about the absolutely supreme way this knowledge was brought home to me.

My oldest son, Bryan needed my car, so he drove me to work. As we were traveling, I told him, "Slow down Bryan, you're going to hit a child." In shock I realized I just verbalized what I had been thinking for far too long. Bryan dropped me off, and I forgot all about this until the next morning when I drove the same route again. As I neared the same spot, I said to myself, "Sharon, slow down, you're going to hit a child." I quickly reasoned with myself that, *if thoughts are things and what you think really does happen*—this means I have been creating a terrible scenario!

Universal Laws teach that each scenario we create must go through the "thought-talk-action" process and thoughts are "fueled" by the emotion behind each one! How many times have I said to myself, "I knew that was going to happen," but I never made the connection that I helped create it! Self-responsibility again?

Immediately, I spend the next eight minutes driving to work, saying out loud, "Dear God," with emotion and gusto in my voice, "I am always a defensive driver; all children are safe around me; I avoid all accidents; etc., etc., etc." I had a fleeting moment when I hoped people would think I was singing along with the radio, if they noticed me. There's that old ego! At the end of my drive to work I added, "You know God, if I ever saw a child get hit, I wouldn't be able to help as I have no medical experience, but I would be there to comfort. Amen." I arrived at work and, as usual, this beseeching prayer no longer occupied my mind. The thoughts were released into the Universe to do their work.

The following week, I left work at 4:15 PM. I worked on Kuller Road, in Clifton; a mile long industrial road. When I left that day, there were about seven or eight boys riding their bikes on both sides of the road. Being familiar with the neighborhood boys in this area and how they liked to play chicken, I slowed down and made sure I drove only as fast as they were peddling.

One of the older boys in front of me looked up the road and back several times before quickly darting in front of my car to the other side of the road. He was playing "chicken." A few seconds later, a younger boy on the left side of highway looked up the road, saw a car coming, then looked back at me, not realizing the car coming at him was going over forty miles an hour and the boy pulled directly into the path of the oncoming car. As we passed each other, I saw a redheaded woman with a look of horror on her face, arching her body on the seat of the car, and standing on her brakes. I will never forget the sound of the screeching, crunching metal!

I immediately pulled over to the right side of the road, as I was in shock! I was talking very fast to myself, "I want to go home; I don't want to be here!" An inner voice gently said, "You were *the* other car." I answered, "I know, but I don't want to be here." Again the voice gently said, "You were *the* other car." Exhausted, I finally slumped down. Instantly, I sensed that the Cosmos used my body as a *Spiritual go-through* although I was yet unaware that my prayers gave a Spiritual cushion for this Karmic happening, and because of those efforts, the child would live."

I got out of my car, running in circles, screaming for someone in the big nearby buildings to call an ambulance, as there were no cell phones at that time. A white van pulled up on the opposite side of the road. The driver got out and said they had been called; immediately I calmed down. I looked behind me about fifty feet, and people were beginning to gather around the child. I slowly walked back, fearing the worst. As I walked around the car, the bike lay in a twisted heap; the boy had been thrown onto a driveway. "Thank God, there was no blood," though his one thigh was turned inside out by a compound fracture. He began to stir. Everyone was standing far away from him. His friend, the oldest boy that crossed over in front of my car said, "Ooh, look at his leg!" The injured boy heard him, looked around, and attempted to roll over. His blood-curdling scream is etched in my brain forever! I immediately walked over to him, although I was warned by several not to touch him. I assured everyone I wouldn't as I knelt down beside him. I placed my hands under his head as a soft cushion, and gently said, "My name is Sharon, and I will stay with you. You've had an accident; you are in one piece but you will have to be checked out at the hospital." The child began to whimper and called for his mother; I assured him she was on her way. This is when I put into practice what I had been taught in Elizabeth's classes. I prayed that God would pass healing, calming energy through me into this child. Finally, the police arrived, followed by the EMTs. Relieved I got up, gave the officer my information, and assured him I would mail in my eyewitness report.

When I turned away from the police officer, I saw the young red headed woman who had been driving the car that hit the boy. She was crying, smoking, and shaking from head to toe; I walked towards her, hugged her close, and gently said, "I was driving *the* other car and I saw everything. There was nothing you could do, he shot directly in front of your car, you could not have stopped in time, and you didn't stand a chance. I will state it all in my police report." She tearfully thanked me and I quickly left. I had a hair appointment to get to.

Every time I blinked my eyes, I heard it, I saw it! "It was such a horror," I told my beautician. Still shaking with the memory, I went home and told my husband Bernie, son Jamie and daughter Jocelynn. Sleep was elusive that night.

The next day, I returned home after work, and my oldest son, Bryan, walked in and I realized he hadn't heard what happened to me, as he had been working the entire evening before. I told him my story, and a funny look appeared on his face. "Mom, we were just talking about that last week," Bryan exclaimed. My head started to buzz. How could I have forgotten those feverish petitions to God the week before; and not only that what about, *If I ever see a child get hit, I don't have any medical experience, but would be there to comfort!"* Was this a Divine setup? WOW! I wonder, was I no more than one week from creating such an accident myself? "From my lips to God's ears!"

## I CHANGED MY HAT

There came a day when my husband Bernie said to me, "You'd better think about how you're changing your whole foundation." I could only murmur, "Thank God!" My foundation told me hate is the opposite of love, but everything has changed for me now and I know that fear is the true opposite of love. We either walk in faith or we walk in fear. Instilling our faith is merely the beginning of the journey, not the end.

I learned something supremely interesting to me in the beginning chapters of Hebrews in the King James Version of the Bible. I used this version because it is the least edited Bible we have. The HEBREWS VI:1 verse states: *Therefore, leaving the principles of the doctrine of Christ, let us go on unto perfection, not laying again the foundation of repentance from dead works and of faith toward God.* I have found in my years of going to the Catholic masses that they don't deviate much. They stay on a certain path through the New Testament, year after year after year, and creatively make up new homilies or sermons about the same information. They read designated

35

parts that lead the whole flock down a preset path of their choosing, not God's. Now, what does this all mean?

To me, this means we are to go from a state of *faith* to a state of *knowing*. When we are encouraged by our religions to remain in a constant state of faith, it is like never getting out of grammar school. We are to continually grow, ever changing, and ever deeper in our concept of what God is, and not stay stuck in one spot forever!

Yep, my life is changing and I learned in my forties how to be more positive; can't really say going to church helped me that much at that time, but we went to church through the 90's because it is something my husband wanted. In the mid-90s, during a late night discussion, Bernie said, "Sharon, I know that what you speak is Truth, but my mother is still alive and it would break her heart if I changed my thoughts now; besides, I like my Catholic hat." I looked at him, grinning and said, "That's fine, but remember it's only a hat and can be changed."

## I AM BUYING A HOUSE

Bernie decided he was going to retire. For me, there is no one that compares to Bernie. He has made a hands-down great policeman and detective because he has great gut feelings and is able to quickly and intelligently react. On the other hand major life changes or major decisions set him back slightly; retiring was definitely one of them. He enjoyed his for-certain future and this retiring and *what am I going to do now* has left him unsure of himself and what he will be doing after retirement. Bernie had been short-tempered with all of us and, when that happens, we all walk a mile around him!

Finally, one weekend I decided to lie down for a short nap, but ole Bern kept popping into my head. Why is he so short with the kids now? Everything seems to be a fight, and I am confused, trying to understand what is going on. I eventually dozed off and when I awoke, lo and behold, in living color in front of me was a vision of Bernie's face grinning from ear to ear! I knew that if I opened my eyes, I would lose this image, so I said, "Lord, this must mean something." It was so vivid; and the voice said, "Ask him," so, I looked into the eyes of his vision and said, "What is the matter with you, why are you so miserable?" Bernie, grinning like a fool, said, "I am buying a house!"

"BINGO," I said to myself! Instantly I got it! It was another BIG life decision and had Bernie more than a little unnerved! He had acted the same way when we bought our first home 1971, and now he was acting this way again because he was on the verge of retiring in 1992. It took this insight for me to finally understand his pattern.

## WHY ARE YOU LIMITING GOD?

Bernie retired in 1993, and while talking one afternoon, he said, "You know Sharon, my retirement has kicked in and all I need is a part time job to earn the same salary I had as a detective." I said, "That's fine, but why are you limiting God?"

He said, "Whaaaaa?" Remembering a story from Elizabeth's classes, I told him, *"It's like a woman who wants to get married, and all she can think of is an Italian stallion to wine and dine her, and of course he will be sexy, have money and be a great dancer. Everyone will admire her catch - especially all the other women!" Everyone ends up loving him; including him! God gives us free will, and allows us to put a fence around what we want. This woman doesn't realize it, but while she is looking for her perfect partner, a shorter man with thinning hair and wearing glasses is walking outside her fence and although she doesn't see him, he would have been the love of her life!"*

I told Bernie every thought is a prayer, I told him God is a creator, and our thoughts become our reality. He asked, "Then how should I pray?" I told him to start thanking God for the:

perfect job,

perfect salary,

perfect distance,

perfect co-workers

In fact these people would be so perfect it would be like a marriage. They would hear him and he would hear them. There would be give and take on both sides.

This job would be so perfect that it would take him into his retirement years, and of course, he couldn't set on his haunches and would need to network as well! Bernie ended up having a wonderful second career and retired after fifteen years. We both re-learned the lesson of setting a condition, focusing, and manifestation, using the well-taught techniques from Elizabeth Joyce's classes.

### YES, BUT ARE YOU SAVED?

I've never understood this! I've had all these outrageous experiences that I cannot explain; does this mean I am saved? I know this is a carry-over from my protestant upbringing, but I often wonder if I'll ever know the answer to this question.

Months passed since my "electric" dream; we were invited to a friend's home along with nine other people for dinner because we were going to attend a "Healing Mass." Our friends had persuaded their local priest to invite a Betty Brennan for this occasion. This Betty Brennan was on a

38

special committee, sanctioned by the Pope. She had the gift of discernment and asked every person a question, pertinent to their life and Spirit. After dinner we attended mass, and at the end of the regular mass, the parish priest exited. When he returned back into the church, the Healing Mass began.

This is one of those *slain in the Spirit* hands on healings. For me, this was the Catholic version of a good ole' protestant revival. The Bible speaks about how Spirit enters the body and when "this" happens; people will collapse in "the Spirit," some even falling on the floor! A "catcher" is there to ease you on down.

I'll cut right to the chase…it's my turn to go up before this Betty Brennan. She was standing beside a priest who traveled with her and he anointed my forehead with oil as I stood in front of the two of them. She stood slightly to my right and takes my right elbow in her left hand and says, "Is there anything I can do for you?" I grin and say, "Nooo, I am here to acknowledge God as the one true and living God, and to thank him for all my obstacles that have made me grow."

She and the priest laughed at me – I laughed too, what the heck, I was very light-hearted about this whole thing. The discerning question she asked me was, "Are you aware of your true value?" I smile widely and say, "Yes, that's what my obstacles have been about." Betty and the priest laughed again, and then she says, "Okay let's pray." As I closed my eyes I saw her place her right hand in front of my heart.

I would like to interject here that many years ago I had a good friend tell me she was saved, but she couldn't explain what had happened. Well, like I said, God has brought me in through the back door. When I have an experience I am compelled to go in search of what happened to me. We have a Universe where everything runs like clockwork; God must have some sort of Universal order and reason for it all.

Anyway, the moment I closed my eyes, something slammed into the top of my head circling down, under and around my heart. It was so forceful, it entered with a roar, and I felt like my head was encased in a thick pillow or a vacuum. I heard Betty praying for me but she sounded muffled and seemed a long distance away, making it impossible to hear her words. I was aware this loud thing was happening inside my head and moving down and around my heart. I couldn't move; I couldn't breathe. What I felt is best described as being electrocuted, pulled up really fast, or being dropped in a runaway elevator! My eyes involuntarily opened just a sliver. Believe me; in no way did I open them! They opened of their own accord! I was being riveted to the spot and had no muscular control. Through the slit, my eyes saw clearly the gold rope design on the priest's vestment in front of me, along with a bright, extremely intense white floodlight shining by the outside corners of my eyes, yet this Light remained inside my eyes. A pure, bright white floodlight is what best describes this light.

The roar, the extremely bright White Light, along with the inability to move or breathe, lasted the entire time Betty prayed over me. When she stopped, the roar and the intense White Light stopped as if someone threw a switch! She asked me if I was okay. "Me, oh sure, I'm fine." I felt like I had just been awakened from a dead sleep. I walked from her thinking, "Dear God, please let me make it," to a man holding a Bible open for the local priest to read a verse. This parish priest anointed me, but I grabbed the gentleman's arm next to me holding the Bible and said, "You gotta gimme a minute, I feel dizzy." When I was composed, the kindly priest read his verse and I began crying. I sobbed to the priest, "That's one of the most beautiful things I've ever heard." As I turned, my friend's husband was there. He was one of those catchers and was behind me because I was apparently shaky, I took his arm and he walked me back to my pew. All I could do was cry and say to him, "You didn't tell me this was gonna happen, you didn't tell me," sob, sniffle.

The next day I realized that anything I have ever experienced absolutely pales in comparison to this. WHAT was it? HOW and WHY did it enter me? What does it MEAN? I am no scholar, but I dig deep and my extensive research tells me this experience is at the center of all our religions, yes, even cults. It can become really involved so I will try to simplify it as much as humanly possible. Real, inner baptism is an actual psychological and Spiritual event.

**In order of longevity:**

In Hinduism, this Light eliminates all negativity and takes one off the wheel of Karma; placing one on the wheel of Grace. It is said that the reincarnation cycle stops and this Light physically changes everything down to the cellular level, even changing the way one will die.

Gnosticism is being included here in honor of heathens, or as they are often referred to, cults. The Gnostic Baptism is sometimes called The Cosmic Baptism, The Baptism of Light, or The Baptism of Fire. In one form or another, the Initiation takes place sometime during one's life, no matter what path one may follow, either in another ritual form or subconsciously.

Buddhism has the Yamas and Niyamas; sins to be mastered and virtues to be embodied and considers this the most powerful experience one can have on this earth.

Judaism talks about the blessing that comes only from approaching God in the proper performance of God's commandments (this is akin to mastering the seven deadly sins in Christian terms). It is referred to as Birkat Kohanim, where the proper, full pronunciation of the word God brings both material and spiritual blessing, and fulfillment of the Divine promise, which is an inner anointing. Study of the Kabala offers deep, inner reflection of the body and Spirit, which can lead one towards the God-experience.

In Christianity it is the *saving* experience or true Baptism, the descent and awakening of the Holy Spirit, and lies at the heart of the Catholic religion, the Protestant Church and Pentecostalism.

Islam associates this with Rohaniat Wahdatul Wajud; a subjective experience, where mystic and object of love become identical and the ultimate realization is Truth.

All Spiritual traditions have this! When the seeker becomes *pure* enough it will manifest. *Pure* is ancient and not the term I would use. To me this is more akin to one taking steps over time to correct the negative side of their thinking while they strive to live a more positive life. I believe it is this experience at the center of the God-pie, and like I stated before, I feel that religion has taken their piece and run with it.

As time goes by, I said to myself, my closest friends and family that, "I really don't know what that experience meant, but I have a feeling that when my life is over I am outta here—don't know where I am going, but I know I am finished with the planet Earth." Now, *why* does this come out of my mouth, and what can it *mean*?

Several years later, I sent away for a *Past Life Reading* from Edgar Casey's Association for Research and Enlightenment in Virginia Beach, VA. I enjoy learning like this and the readings are based on Edgar's reincarnation information, gleaned from his ability to go into a trance and connect with the God/Super Consciousness/Universal Hall of Records. Believe me, it took years, but I've relinquished all fear from my youth that these beliefs are evil.

Finally the reading arrives. It was loaded with information but then I read a paragraph about myself that still fills me with wonder, "You will have the ability in this lifetime to experience God in many different ways, and if you do it correctly, you will literally leave the Solar System." Suddenly, I had a clue as to where I might be going "when this life is over and I'm outta here!"

In the two religions I've spent time experiencing, we were taught that God is Light; well, I've had the experience and for me, this has the ring of Truth. After all my research, I found within the New Testament of the Bible, St. John, 3:2 where Jesus is talking with Nicodemus. Please read this for yourself because here I give you my rendition:

Nicodemus said, *"Jesus, God must be in you or you couldn't do these miracles,"* (I muse that maybe he is asking how he can do these things).

Jesus says, *"You must be born again."*

Nicodemus says, *"What am I supposed to do, jump back inside my mother?"*

Jesus said, *"No, there is a physical birth and there is a Spiritual birth. When you are born of the Spirit, it is a wind that enters from you know not where, and thou hearest the sound thereof, but canst not tell whence it cometh, and whither it goeth, so is every one that is born of the Spirit."*

Oh My God!!! This described my own experience!

Why do we have such division if God is God? Truly God is the whole pie; man is the divider and, thankfully, I no longer confuse God with religion. When really thought out, each is nothing more than a theory! We all work from edited, loose-leaf religious texts and if all our scriptures were truly the "word of God," don't you think they would at least agree? It seems to me they are more the "word of man," and far too open to interpretation. There is not a single belief system big enough to individually possess everything about this Supreme energy we call God. If God is worth his salt, he will be there for the Eskimo in the igloo as well as the native in the hut! No one has to save anyone! God is more than big enough to get this job done. I firmly believe our religions need God. God does not need our religions.

Church did not lead me to this experience—obviously, it does for some. For me it was all those years of reflection, contemplation, meditation and deep prayer. I know others who've had this experience seemingly *out of the blue* because they are able to describe exactly what I experienced. It frightens some; others begin going to church or, if they were churchy, they go more; some, like me, stop. Whatever you choose to do, your life can never be the same again. In retrospect, I am at peace, at ease, and connected wherever I am, whether in mosque, church, temple, ashram, sweat lodge, work, home, or Shop-Rite, etc.

## MY AT-HOME ALTAR

In the spring of 1991, I felt God wanted me to set up a place in my home where I could pray. I asked mother how to make an altar; she suggested a small spot where I would place my Bible, a candle and a rose; for some reason this didn't thrill me.

One weekend, I mentioned this to my close friend Mary, at our summer get-a-way and she suggested, "Ask God for one." I liked this idea more and implemented it during my next prayer session; along with the request it be affordable. Wouldn't you know, the "very" next weekend, Bernie and I are up at our summer get-a-way, bouncing around a few garage sales when, as I am walking into one, I spied something on the floor.

The man who was running the sale was speaking with a woman. I walked inside the garage before I was able to say, "Excuse me Mister, how much is your altar?" He bodily turns toward me saying, "What?" I knew I had shocked him, so I down-played it. "Umm, that religious thing on the floor." How thrilled was I when he said, "One dollar."

I cart home my new/old plaster of Paris altar to our summer place and put it on our sofa after cleaning it up. It's rather large, made of white chalk ware, with a Last Supper design across the front. This one has the sacred-heart of Jesus on the top and there are twelve glass candles that pull up. WOW! It even lights up!

I called my friend Mary over. I didn't tell her and when she walked inside the summer trailer, she grinned at me and said, "You found your altar!"

"For sure!" I warmly responded.

## ENERGY HEALING

I was fortunate to work for a company I loved for thirteen years. I cared deeply for each and every one working there and even cared about the vendors who frequently stopped by. There were several weeks when women vendors, along with women I worked with, spoke to me about their children and how guilty they felt about leaving their children and not being at home.

At home on the 7th of June, 1994; after dinner, I told Bernie I felt like God wanted me to pray for the mothers of the world who were so guilt ridden because they had to leave their babies in day care. I asked Bernie to man the phones and I went upstairs for about forty-five minutes. I entered our bedroom where I had my at-home altar set up in a corner, I shut the door, lit a candle, closed my eyes and began to pray.

First, I went down the list of the women that had come to my attention, then I blessed the women on my street, in my town, city, state, country, world, and beyond. After I was finished with the mothers, I began praying for my family. I spent time on each one, but when I mentioned Bryan's name (our oldest son), something way out of the ordinary happened; Bryan's image appeared before me! He was about eight inches tall and in living color. There was something very strange about the vision, because a dark, gray cloud encircled his head and chest.

I knew if I opened my eyes, this image would disappear, so I said out loud, "Lord, that's not right, let's get rid of the shadow. Let's put in green light (the color of healing), pink (the color of love), and white (the color of truth)." With eyes closed, I fanned the air in front of me; and blew the cloud away. When the dark cloud was gone, I said, "That's better Lord." I finished up by praying for all those I love, the ones I know and don't know. As usual, when it was over, I thought nothing more of this experience.

The next day, at 4:15 PM, at work, I received a call from a nurse in Hackensack Hospital. She told me Bryan had been in an accident. This nurse was wonderful, assuring me, "Bryan can see, think, hear, breathe, and speak, though he has bodily injuries that will need to heal." She cautioned, "Mother, take your time driving here, keep both hands on the wheel because your son Bryan is okay."

Bernie and I met at the hospital and heard about the freak dirt bike accident our twenty-one year-old son had been involved in. Bryan couldn't get a regular dirt bike, so he borrowed a friend's small motorcycle and attempted to jump on a homemade metal ramp somewhere in the Meadowlands with this heavy bike. The ramp acted like a springboard throwing our Bryan and the bike up into the air! He came down and the heavy bike landed on top of him!

Bryan had clavicle, wrist, hip, and ankle injuries and everything over time did indeed heal. Our life revolved around Bryan and his needs for a while and it was several days before I even had a chance to recall that "cloud of gray" I saw encircling his upper body. I was as *sure* God worked through me to heal my son and prevent serious injuries as well, because I *knew* Bryan could have experienced head, neck or spinal cord injury. The surprise for me was the realization that in praying for the mothers of the world, I ultimately prayed for myself!

## MUFFIN, MY NEW GUARDIAN ANGEL

I learned at the knee of my guru, Elizabeth Joyce, that when you are ready for new energy, you can bless and release your current Guardian Angel or guides to go where they are most needed. Because of my Spiritual growth, I decided I must surely be ready. (Is that my ego again?) I said a sincere prayer thanking God, my angels, and guides for their service, and released them so they could go on to those who needed them at this time. I felt I was ready for new energy along with some new guides, to come into my life.

May I interject that this happened when Bernie and I were married twenty-six years. We made it past the early, rough part of our marriage and rebuilt on a new, solid foundation. Many times I have blessed and continue to bless, all our family and friends who listened, encouraged, and loved us through this turbulent growing spurt. Bernie and I found our help in therapy and marriage counseling, which transformed our marriage from a negative to a positive experience. Occasionally, we sometimes fall back into these ancient patterns until one of us realizes an old sleeping dragon has raised its ugly head.

Three weeks after my prayer, Bernie and I had a nasty argument about 10:00 PM on a Friday evening. I chose to leave his company and go to bed. Around 11:30 PM Bernie came up to bed and fell asleep, and that's when I woke up. I could not get back to sleep. I began to dialogue, "God, I don't know what's the matter, Bern is not happy and neither am I. What's causing us to act like this?" Heavens, I was up for hours thinking, praying, and pondering. In the midst of pouring out my heart, I thought, "I just don't know what the problem is!" Suddenly a voice interrupted, saying, "You're dealing with a faceless woman." My instinctual reply, "What the hell is a 'faceless' woman?"

I knew I had been blessed with another voice so about 2:00 AM, I got out of bed and went downstairs, pulled out a mindless book and began to read/think/read/think for three more hours until I was exhausted. Within that time I began realizing exactly why Bernie and I were so unhappy and "the faceless woman" began to make perfectly good sense. There wasn't an actual woman threatening our marriage, but it's the woman Bernie wishes I would be! He would like me to clean our home like one of our very good friends; to have the perfect figure, like another of our friends; he wished I would play golf with him; having long nails like so-n-so would be nice too…etc., etc., etc. This is the 'woman of his dreams!' Shoot, a live woman would be easier to handle! "Lord, how am I supposed to deal with a woman who is not real?" I crept back to bed around 5 AM, mentally and physically exhausted.

I'm dreaming. I'm in a huge department store walking into the open concourse. I stopped and stared because everything was glass, white and shiny. A tall, slim, long-legged black woman with a short Afro, wearing white short-shorts was walking straight towards me. As she neared me, she looked straight into my eyes, smiled and said, "Hi, my name is Muffin and I will help you." I came up from this dream giggling, saying to myself, "A muffin is one of my most favorite things." My eyes flew open! "Oh my God, I have been given the strength of a black woman!"

Far too long it's been apparent to me that numerous generations of black women have suffered through countless travesties, made to be strong from unspeakable horror and suffering. I was filled with emotion and cried quietly; thanking God for this wonderful blessing of the new strength I was given. Bernie began stirring and said he's going to get up. I told him I will join him in a few minutes. When he was out of our bedroom, I began talking directly to Muffin. I told her, "We are going in there to talk to Bernie and tears cannot be a part of this."

I joined him in the shower. Over the years, it's been a great place for us to talk things out because it's hard to get angry and leave when you aren't wearing anything. I entered the shower and he's standing there, waiting patiently, arms folded. He said, "What took you so long?" I told him that I only had three hours sleep; my agony about our apparent unhappiness, and realization of old, unhealthy patterns that were surfacing again, BUT, I told him, there has been another voice. Within this voice was the answer to my agonies because it told me I was "dealing with a faceless woman."

Bern looked at me and said, "What the hell is a faceless woman?"

"Those were my exact words too," I replied.

Here is what I discovered." You *would like me to clean our home like one of our very good friends; to have the perfect figure, like another of our friends; you wished I would play golf with you; having long nails like so-n-so would be nice too...etc., etc., etc. This is the woman of your dreams!*

When I finished, he said, "Well, if this is true it isn't your problem, it's mine." I agreed. I assured him of my very deep love for him and said, "I am setting you free to go and put a face on that woman. If that face isn't my face then I love you enough to let you go, because if you ain't happy, I ain't happy."

There weren't any tears on my part. Thank you Muffin! When the shower was over we went about our day and it wasn't mentioned again. Several days later he brought me flowers and eighteen years later, in 2012, we celebrated our forty-fourth wedding anniversary!

## BARNSTORMING HEAVEN

A woman I worked with for a good ten years was relocating with her family to Florida. Her son would start college there and they decided to move lock, stock and barrel! This woman's work ethic was over-the-top as far as her dedication goes. Over the years, our company had moved her into every department and she ended up overseeing the entire plant. She was amazing. She stood at my front desk and we were talking; I told her that since she was going to be beginning again in a new area; she could relax and hand-pick where she wanted to work. She didn't skip a beat but flat-out told me it wouldn't matter if she worked in a diner, she would work as if she owned it! As I listened to her, I realized how she had aged and if she didn't learn to relax, her health would not last, so I began every morning to barnstorm God with prayers for my friend. Week one, week two, week three, week four, oh my heavens, tomorrow is her last day!

That morning I got the kids off to school, sat down at the kitchen table to read, reflect and pray. I talked earnestly, beseechingly, bemoaning to God. I prayed: "Oh Lord, it's her last day and there's been no difference. She's leaving this weekend. Please Dear God, please, open her eyes and ears. Dear Lord, how can there be a difference if she doesn't see?" I thought, "Amen."

Another good friend and I took her out for lunch and her last day slipped by. About four o'clock, she came over to my desk, plopped all her books and ledgers down and said, "Something just happened to me!" I had my back to her because I was typing. I continued typing but leaned my right ear back towards her as she spoke.

She told me she went into the computer room to chat with the data-entry girl and described how they were laughing and talking when all of a sudden somebody came in with a problem and the data-entry girl went from zero to ten in one second, got red in the face, and started screaming and cursing! My friend continued, "For the first time my eyes were opened and I saw myself! The data entry girl was doing just fine until the problem walked in; and that's exactly how I would have reacted!"

I spun around, grabbing her arm, "What did you say?" Surprised, she repeated it for me. I shared with her that I had been praying for her for one month and she said the exact words I had prayed that very morning. I further explained how I had seen her age during our years together, and when she and her husband settled in Florida, if she didn't slow down, her pace would begin affecting her health.

After a year my co-worker, Eileen and I flew down to Florida to see our friend. I don't know for sure, but I bet our company needed to hire several workers to replace her! She ended up choosing a part time accounting job for a podiatrist and loved it! She told us that when they moved she thought she would be all right after a couple of months but, in reality, she said it took almost a full year for her body to heal. She had pushed herself so hard.

Man, it just doesn't get any better than that!

## SACRED HOLOGRAMS

We had a summer place for twenty-five years while the kids were growing up. We started with a small trailer and about every seven years we would buy a larger one to accommodate our growing family. I deeply loved this campsite. We didn't have TV so our kids learned to enjoy nature and be creative on their own. I think for all of us this special place was a true respite.

As our kids became teens, I found myself with more time for reading, meditating and praying. Woods surrounded us and Bernie and I did our best to keep the atmosphere low key; you know, no bright lights at night or loud noises other than us! So often there, I felt we were nuzzled within the heart of nature.

One day, mid 90's, I was alone for a good long while; kids were out gallivanting; Bernie was golfing and I eagerly set myself up on the sofa next to a large window with my cassette player to enjoy a one-hour meditation. That day I chose a tape called, *Fear-less*, put my earphones on, and allowed my mind to calm down. As I meditated, I opened my eyes once in a while to gaze out the window at our beautiful, tall trees and I mused, "Thank you trees for your years of shade and protection, thank you that you withstood the violent thunderstorms and didn't fall on us." I also loved each rock and boulder, so I thanked them too for their support, then the ants and mice, thank you for never invading our space, when suddenly; a voice interrupted my reverie and said, "We are grateful you never hurt us." After I recovered from being startled, I was filled with *gratitude* knowing the life force in the surrounding nature was just as grateful for us as we were for all of them.

As I continued listening to the cassette, I got to the part where the woman whispered, "My heart opens to love." In my mind I am picturing how I would draw this. Would it be as a cutesy heart with flowers around it, or maybe a real heart with real flowers bursting forth? Often I lazily opened and shut my eyes. One time as I opened them, before me I saw my first sacred hologram! It was two angels, or guides? These two didn't have wings; they were transparent and they were males because they had flat chests, so I reasoned that made them guides. The first one was closest to me sitting in a chair; the second male stood behind him a little to his right; they both wore white robes. I was in such a state of relaxation, my eyes gently closed and just as quickly they flew open; they were gone! Can you believe they were larger than the ceiling in my trailer, in white, long robes; the one standing had a loose belt around his waist, and they were both watching me! This halted my meditation in its tracks. I got up, pulled out a divination game using a regular deck of cards. I said a short prayer asking God a question; "Who were they?" Would you believe, when I laid out the cards, one of the sayings was, "You are being watched by a doctor from the other side." Am I? Who knows, but several of my neighbors called me the 'Witch Doctor of Monona Avenue," because of my interest in different methods of healing.

Later that evening, I prepared dinner for our friends, Mary and Bill, who stayed in the campsite across from us. I absolutely loved them. Bill was mechanical and Mary was interested in plants, animals, everything within nature! Bernie would show Mary any treasure he found while hiking with the kids, and she would bring back little, unknown plants she found while walking her pit bull, Bubbles, in the forest. They always tried to figure out just what plants they found and what they could be used for.

Mary had hurt her back, and I wanted her to relax, so we invited them over for dinner. Mary and Bernie were carrying on an animated conversation while I sat, very relaxed, gazing up at Mary's face, when suddenly her features changed right before my eyes!! I saw my second sacred hologram that day! Mary's hair darkened, her face elongated, she had high cheekbones and her jaw became very square. The only things that remained the same were her beautiful blue eyes. I immediately snapped to attention and she was back to her old self, but I had been given the realization that we knew each other in another lifetime, long ago. She had a definite male, Indian-look and it explained her love of nature and all things wild in this lifetime as far as I was concerned.

Can't ever say I've experienced a day like this one! One for the books!

## HOLY CRAZINESS!  CRAZY HOLINESS!

Maybe it's his voice; maybe it's the words that come through him, but as Elton John's songs deepened during the 90's, they often touched the deepest part of my heart and soul.

On a Friday, sometime in the fall of 1996, I was driving to work on the industrial road leading to the office when a song came on the radio—Elton John's "*Baby, You're the One*." These lyrics hit me right in the solar plexus: "When stars collide like you and I, no shadows block the sun; you're all I've ever needed, Baby you're the one."

Filled instantly with emotion (devotion?), I pulled over on the side of the road and dedicated this song to God. I told God, "This love we share is stronger than the love I feel for my husband or my family." As usual, I said "Amen," forgot about it and went about my day.

In the middle of the night, I woke up needing to go to the bathroom; I was half asleep and especially groggy; it was so dark that I collided with the door jam … ugh!  I was literally in mid-descent, concentrating on zeroing in on the toilet seat, when a voice interrupted me with; "I am going to take Bernie from you."  I flopped down on the john and thought, "Oh Lord, my Bernie."  I crept back to bed, but sleep was finished for me.

The next day, Saturday afternoon, we were to spend the day with good friends of ours, Mike and Pat. Bernie and Mike were going golfing, and I was to hang with my friend Pat until they returned. When Bernie and I arrived at their home, I was told Pat would be late because of a changed hair appointment. The men left and in the silence, my downward spiral grew stronger, and descended into fear. By the time Pat arrived, I was in the midst of a major fear meltdown. She did her best to calm me, helping me sort

55

through my confusion, and somehow I managed to regain some semblance of *normalcy*. However, it would be almost impossible to shake the fear of losing my husband.

Monday morning arrived and while on my way to work, the exact same song by Elton John played again on the car radio! Quickly, I pulled over to the side of the road, asking myself, "What made me feel I wanted to dedicate this song to God?" Like a jolt, I remembered soon enough it was when Elton John sang the words, *"When stars collide, like you and I; no shadows block the sun, you're all I've ever needed, Baby, you're the one."*

This was the exact point in the song when I made my dedication to God, "This love we share is stronger than the love I feel for my husband and family ... Boy, oh, boy, it seems this was not altogether true, and the "Big Guy" needed to show me my love and dedication wasn't directed exactly where I thought it was! My entire waste line was sore from the tension I held over this past weekend. Without reservation, I *knew* my love was dedicated to my immediate family. I had a huge regret when I realized I'd received a swift kick from God squarely in my stomach!

## OUR MIRACLE IN HOLLAND

In June of 1997, I slipped and fell hard in the middle of a street. While on the ground, a thought flipped through my mind that I had three months to heal before we would leave on our trip to Europe. By the next morning, I had to go to the hospital where I learned I had a broken right ankle, left elbow, and eventually found out I also severed the left rotator cuff. I had the option of a cast, but it was summer so I opted to stay off my feet and not have casts. In July, my body threw a kidney stone because I was so sedentary. I naively believed I had passed the stone when, after drinking gallons of water, the pain stopped.

The rotator was repaired in August, and after resting two weeks I began six weeks of physical therapy. It was determined by the doctors that I could to go on our vacation to Europe as planned, before returning back to work.

Exactly six days before we were to fly to Europe in October, I had a large showing of blood in the urine, so on Monday I quickly went to my urologist. He scheduled a sonogram on Wednesday that determined I had never passed the kidney stone that now needed to be removed surgically. The surgeon worked with us, removed the stone Friday evening, but had to place a tube in my urethra because of the swelling the stone created. The doctor warned me my body would expel this tube within two or three days. He armed me with an antibiotic, anti-spasm medication, and his home phone number. The next morning Bern and I winged our way across the pond to Holland. Leave it to me, a dumb Pisces, *"I am never afraid to go wherever the Universe leads me."*

Being definitely determined, but not a total fool, my activities each morning in Holland were limited, combined with resting the remaining three-quarters of each day. I missed seeing most of Amsterdam. In the wee hours, around 2:00 AM on our last night in Amsterdam, it became apparent the stint was going to expel. We were both relieved. I took my anti-spasm meds and Bernie went back to sleep. All too quickly I began having the most intense and urgent feelings I have ever experienced of "having to go." I began drinking a large bottle of water. If I gave in to these urgent urges, I would never leave the "john." I figured out a schedule and each time, after going to the bathroom, I'd chug down another large bottle of water. I sat on the edge of the bed, crossing my arms in front of my breasts, rocking to and fro while not taking my eyes off the clock in front of me. I mentally counted the slow moving twenty-five minutes, when I could, at last go and there would be 'something' to come out. The continual cramping was almost unbearable.

Understand I am no baby when it comes to pain This was intense! Somewhere around 4:00 AM I thought to myself, "When is this anti-spasm medication going to kick in?" Shocked I soon realized, "it isn't going to ... and I am in deep trouble!" I kept up this twenty-five minute drinking, counting, rocking regimen until Bernie woke up at 5:30 AM, because he had to make a bathroom run himself. While he's gone, I moved from the edge of our bed to the edge of a small chair facing the bed. When Bernie returned, I told him what had been going on, and he asked, "Is this something we are going to have to address in the morning?" I told him, "If this is still happening, I will have to go to the hospital." It was just before dawn and so dark in our room I could barely make out his outline.

I closed my eyes and began the rocking and counting regimen again; when I opened my eyes—it's still dark and ever so hard to see Bernie, though I can tell his right hand is extended towards me. I thought to myself, "Ooooh Lord, Bernie is praying for me." Comforted, I closed my eyes and began silently repeating, "I accept, I accept, I accept," to every pulse of my pain, and each beat of my rocking motion. Instantly, a vision of a cloud of gray rolled into my right temple floating gently across my brain. My body slumped, finally relieved of pain. I said to myself, "Oh Lord, I think I can sleep now." I crawled into bed beside Bernie, he reached over to comfort me and I whispered, "don't touch me, don't touch me, I think I can sleep now." I knew the gray cloud had been sent from Spirit to relinquish this intense, painful ordeal, and sleep I did.

At nine-thirty in the morning, sunshine filled our room and I woke up without pain! I ran into the bathroom and this time, nothing hurt – no more intense, unrelenting, cramping urges! It was finished. When I came out of the bathroom, in joy and amazement I looked at my husband and said, "Bernie, all was normal!!" I stood there smiling like an idiot when suddenly I remembered what happened in the wee hours. I looked at Bernie in reverie and asked, "Are you aware of what happened this morning?" Smiling back, Bernie looked at me and said, "I was going to ask you if you were aware something happened."

Oh my!

## ROLLING PIN ENERGY

Bernie and I were invited to join our friends, Mike and Pat, for a weekend at the shore. The home belonged to Mike's aunt, now deceased, and was to be sold at the end of the summer. There was not much furniture so we brought along two wooden army cots that we had picked up years before at a house sale.

At the end of the day, Bern and I turned in for the evening. Bernie wanted our two cots close, so we pushed them together, Bernie removed my pillow and put his arm there for me to use. We were talking when he says, "Sharon, take several deep breaths and relax, I'm going to send energy to a part of your body." I did so, and Bernie says, "Okay, here goes!" Suddenly I felt a sensation as if someone on the inside of me was using a rolling pin and rolled down my back and into my thighs. I giggled, and Bernie asked me, "What's the matter?" I explained I felt something like a rolling pin, rolling down the inside of my back and into my legs. He jerked his arm out, causing me to hit my head on the wooden cot, and said, "Don't say that!" "Why," I asked, rubbing my head; he said, "I sent energy to your knees."

After that energetic experiment, he and I played this "energy" game in restaurants. He would send me energy—

I'd close my eyes, calm myself, and wait until I felt something in some part of my body. It would be a cold, hot, tingly, or prickly feeling. Bernie and I got pretty good at this. As I lowered my head and centered myself, he would write on a napkin where he would be sending energy, and I nailed it much more often than not! Ahhh, what a connection!

## THE OUTRAGEOUS PLATE

Several years after Joe, our friend at the summer camp, passed away we received an invitation to his daughter Denise's wedding, and indeed looked forward to attending this happy event. On a Saturday, one week before the wedding, Bernie and I went out antiquing and in one shop my eyes landed on an old 1908 calendar plate advertising the owner's name and his store. What a coincidence! The owner of the store had the same name as my friend, Joe. It is a rare last name, and in eight more days we will be attending his daughter's wedding! It wasn't as if this was a common last name. As I looked at the old 1908 advertising plate, low and behold the days of the current year were the same as the days on the plate. I became aware that Denise's wedding day fell on the same day and date as shown on this plate. I ignored the strong gut feeling to buy the plate and ended up leaving the store without it.

All week, the plate was on my mind, so I said a prayer, "God, if you want Joe's daughter to have this plate, I promise you I will go back and buy it. Amen, and please don't let anyone else purchase it." During that week I told one of my co-workers, Annie, this story and she's gave me a box from her vast plate collection so I even had a nice display box to put the plate in if I was able to purchase it. When I returned to the antique store the day before Denise's wedding, not only was the plate still there, it was on sale!

On the day of Denise's wedding, I was sitting at my kitchen table wrapping it. These things that happen to me are very unconventional, and my very conventional husband has made me feel this is one of the dumbest things we could ever give a bride. After he gave his song and dance, he went out in the back yard to do some yard work. I knew this plate was very special, yet his strong comments made me feel uncertain, as I forgot the old plate had her father's exact name, Denise's wedding day and date lined up with the day and date on the plate, and I even got it on sale! All pales all because my husband's opinion had made me question myself. There I am, sitting at the table feeling sad, talking to God about this entire situation. "Maybe Bernie is right; giving the plate is a foolish thing to do. Suddenly a voice interrupted my thoughts and said, "Joe smiles." These words were not mine and this intrusive thought was not the way I would word it anyway! "Hmmm," Joe smiles.

My decision became firm! I went outside and told Bernie there was no further debate because I just heard another voice. I was told, 'Joe *smiles*,' and if Joe smiles then Denise gets the plate!" I felt I was the messenger to Denise, bringing her the news that her father and my friend, Joe, approved of her marriage. Later, Denise, in her thank you note to us, called it an "outrageous plate," and it certainly was that!

### ZIP MY LIP!

Oh, heaven help my good friends; it is obvious that my ever-deepening Spirituality is my passion! I felt these Spiritual experiences I was having were over the edge and my concept of what God really is...is ever-changing and growing. My joy overflowed and as I looked back, I realized that Spirituality has dominated a large part of my conversations with my good friends in fact; I am amazed that my friends are still my friends.

There were wonderful friends who lived diagonally across the street from us; Bernie and I loved both Eileen and Harry along with their families. Our husbands had a once a month card game for fifteen or more years with the same group of friends. Generally, the wives would try to get together and go out. It seemed every time I went out with Eileen, I started talking about what I was learning and, even though it got late and her eyes drooped, she never asked me to leave.

I had acted this way several times to her, and lo and behold, she had invited me over to spend another evening with her while our husbands gathered for the card game. I made a prayer and I told God that, *"I promise I won't talk or over-talk about God or Spirituality this time because I don't want my dear friend to get bored from my incessant chatter, in fact, I will let Eileen lead the conversation. Amen."*

When I went over to her home, she asked if I would like to take a walk around the park that was near us. We walked and I let the conversation go wherever she wanted it to, and we returned just as her young teenagers were coming home. She got them some food and asked me if I would like some coffee. As she was preparing it she said, "Oh, I could ask you!" "About what," I replied. Eileen goes on to describe a 'White-Light' experience she had while sitting in church and what did I think about it. Zipping my lip surely is good for me, but I can imagine God had a good laugh at my shock as our evening together unfolded. I proceeded to joyfully give a detailed explanation to her experience.

## OM MANI PADME HUM

I was given this mantra by my guru/teacher Elizabeth Joyce, and I used this Buddhist mantra often because the words are not in English and my mind doesn't get distracted by them. I remember asking her what it meant and she said one meaning is, *"My heart is in the hand of God."*

One day while driving home after a hectic day at work, I was using the mantra to help calm my mind. I was repeating it, breathing in and out, for about eight or nine minutes when, as I entered onto a highway I glanced up at the sky. Immediately, I pulled over to the side of this busy road and got out of my vehicle because there above me was a huge cloud shaped exactly like a heart sitting on a pillow. I marveled as I stood there watching until it lost its shape. Somewhere in my youth I remembered learning from Bible studies that our thoughts can change the wind. I don't remember hearing anything about clouds!

## ANGEL IN A BOOKSTORE

One evening I was out with friends for dinner; not wanting the evening to end, I asked the girls if they wanted to go to our new local bookstore. No one took me up on it so I moseyed on over by myself. As I was checking out all the bargains, I heard an announcement over the loudspeaker that a lecture on angels was about to begin. I quickly went up the escalator and was amazed to find all the seats and floor space taken with standing room only - three people deep! I found a spot where I could barely see over two tall young men's shoulders.

The woman speaking was a local psychic from Elmwood Park, NJ, and she said, "Rather than tell you about what I do, I will show you." She went on to say she would energetically scan the room; which she did. She pointed in our direction to call someone forth; people started to separate and she said, "…more." Finally, the two young men in front of me separated and I was looking at everyone looking at me! Surprised, I said, "Me?" She nodded. I walked into the middle of the room. She asked, "Do you pray a lot?" I replied, "All the time!" She quipped, "You must, because you have the biggest angel in the room shrouding you!" She proceeded to give me a very personal, albeit accurate, psychic reading in front of a packed crowd. What an experience!

### AM I DOING WHAT I NEED TO DO?

Once again, I was questioning myself in a prayer. "Dear God, am I where I need to be, am I doing what I need to do, am I helping enough people? If not, put me where I need to be!" It is my fervent desire to serve and uplift all who enter my energy field.

My dear friend Betsy and I decided to go to a book signing and meet the author of book, whose title escapes me now. The author was from Spain and spoke well, although in broken English. He traveled with several people that coached him from the sidelines telling him the words he struggled for, as he gave his presentation to the group that gathered to hear him.

He told of his youth when his psychic abilities kicked in, and how he knew things that a child should not know. This man looked kind of like Father Time. He was in a light beige colored suit and had a long, white beard. His words were wonderful, and the longer he talked, the more I sat there grinning from ear to ear. Once in a while he smiled and nodded at me. Heaven alone knows what he was must have thought of a woman who couldn't contain her ear-to-ear grin! The things he said really touched my heart.

When he was finished, Betsy bought his book and we hooked arms and got in line for the signing. We were both standing in front of him, saying how much we enjoyed his talk, and as we turned to leave, he took hold of my elbow and said, "I need to tell you that you are doing what you need to do and you will help many, many people." I thanked him. We turned, walked into the book isles as emotion welled up within me and tears ran down my face. What's *this* about? Why did he say *that*? I was walking ahead of Betsy and when I turned around, she said, "Sharon, what's the matter?" I told her I didn't know. It took several more days before I remembered my prayer in the middle of the night and connected it with the realization this man had answered my fervent prayer!

### JOCELYNN'S AURA

Our daughter Jocelynn, at age twenty-one, came to me as I was sitting at our kitchen table; she opened up to me about some pretty upsetting stuff going on in her life. I realized she was too young to be this anxious, and within a couple of days she began therapy to help her sort out why she was having anxiety attacks. A real plus was we began to talk a lot.

One Wednesday, Jocelynn called me at work, deeply upset, and asked me what she could do about an unhealthy situation happening with an old friend. I called AA to find a local support group and was told an Al-A-Non group would be more appropriate. It so happened a local support group was meeting that night near where Jocelynn worked. I quickly called her and she told me she would attend that evening with another one of her friends.

That evening, it was my turn to host a group of women who became friends because of our similar interest in all things of a deeper level. We had met years before at a course offered by the adult school in my town and we got along so well that by the end of the 1990's, we had been meeting in each others homes every other week for eight years. My dear friend Betsy grew up able to see auras and about one hour before our group was over, Jocelynn and her girlfriend came bouncing in. I hadn't told anyone about Jocelynn's adventure and when the two girls came in; Jocelynn gave me the high sign and signaled she would, "Talk to me later." Then they bounced up the stairs.

I was sitting on a sofa next to Betsy when she asked, "What's going on with Jocelynn?" I told her briefly that she had been very anxious, and she said, "Oh, that's good because her aura is so tight against her body, I didn't know if she was too emotional about something or if she was becoming ill." Love that Betsy!

## EXCUSE ME, PLEASE!

In December 1997, we gathered at my eighty-six year old mothers-in-law for dinner. Bernie and I, along with his older brother, wife and daughter were there because she was going into the hospital to have vascular surgery on her leg. In the late afternoon, everyone left, but Bernie and I lingered as his Mom started talking about her life, her mother, father, etc. I was deeply immersed in her memories when a voice suddenly interrupted my reverie saying, "Pray for your mother-in-law." I ignored this interruption and continued listening to these wonderful stories that I had never heard in my thirty-plus years in this family. A while later, the second message came, "Pray for your mother-in-law." "Humph," said I, as I slipped back under the spell of her stories. The third time I was interrupted, "Pray for your mother- in-law," I turned my face away from Bernie and his mother and silently addressed this voice, "God, I promise you I will pray for my mother-in-law before I leave, now please leave me alone so I can enjoy her stories."

When she finished, I sensed we would soon be leaving, so I asked if she minded if I said a prayer over her leg; she nodded her assent. I knelt before her on the floor; Bernie stood beside her and I began to pray. I thanked God for her wonderful leg that had walked so many miles, and then went on to bless the surgeon and everyone else involved. When finished, I looked up and she was deeply looking into my eyes, so deeply that I felt she was looking through me, or at the very least looking into my heart and Soul. Is it possible that, at my age, no one has ever looked so deeply into my eyes? I sensed that she was in a trance, when suddenly she leaned forward to give me a kiss. Whoa! She was going to kiss me on the mouth! I managed to turn my head slightly; she had never done anything like this before! Our mouths met at the corner, as she came out of her trance. As we left I hugged her and told her how much I loved her.

On the way home I told Bernie there's been another voice and that, "Something *big*, something *major* happened back there but I didn't know what." As I spoke my thoughts to him, I said, "Maybe in this lifetime I was here to learn to love your mother enough to pray for her or, maybe we were put here on earth to learn to love and value each other."

I could not possibly have had any idea that this would be my final visit with her, and I am still saddened whenever I think how I turned from her kiss, but then, I'm always comforted when I remember her deep loving look that said, without words, that she knew I loved her enough to pray for her.

### INSTRUSIVE PRAYER

I was once told, by a very wise friend, *"Two of the hardest things you will ever do in this life will be to bury your parents."* Got that right! Our deeply religious mother didn't have an easy time, but nestled within her passing was one of my greatest Spiritual lessons.

Mother was transported home from hospital because she wanted to die in my sister's loving home. Mother had wanted to die for a full year, and when her doctor told us, "Maybe she has a week," we brought her home. My sister and I gathered our immediate families around us. During that early afternoon, my daughter Jocelynn came to me and said, "Mom, this is nothing I've seen, but I sense six or seven angels are gathered on the stairway. They are giving the family this time with Granny because they are taking her tonight." I went upstairs to tell mother and because she was so ready to make this transition; she raised her hands heavenward in prayer praising and thanking God.

In retrospect this would normally have been shocking because Jocelynn, at this time in her life, didn't even want to talk about *this kind of stuff.* That afternoon, my sister and I were in mother's bedroom and she was on her side asleep, facing the wall. I was standing facing her back, with my hands extended towards her praying. My prayer was, "God, please take my mother easily and gently." Suddenly, she raised her head, looked over her shoulder at me and said words that still made me quiver. She said, "Are you praying over me? Oh, God, what did I do to deserve such agony?"

My sister cuts me a look, puts her hands up and says, "Sharon, this is all yours, I'll have no part in it!" Literally, the breath was knocked out of me as I stood there wondering just what it was I had done that was so wrong! Mother did indeed die in the wee hours of the next morning and her passing was anything but easy. Within hours what she said to me began to make perfect sense. Our mother had a lifelong love and devotion for the Lord Jesus, God, and the Bible. She had been a believer ever since she was a six-year-old child and had the "saving" experience. Over the years, as her body weakened, I believe mother became upset with Jesus when, after a lifetime of deep faith, daily devotion, and love, she wasn't healed. She railed against God to my nephews, David and Matt, and I know Matt, the youngest one, was deeply instrumental in helping our mother release her deep anger and disappointment. Later, he told his mother and me that he didn't know where it came from, but he was inspired to say, "Granny, your whole life you've never really suffered; you're suffering now! Do you choose God over your pain?"

Mother's flailing and high anxiety immediately relaxed and she made her decision to choose God over her pain and everything was all over in the next three hours. Remember the analogy of the quilt? We see one side, but only God knows how the threads connect on the other side. There are some things we are not meant to know or understand, but as far as my prayer for my mother goes, I believed she had a decision to make on a deep Soul level, and my intrusive prayer request to "take her easily and gently" did not fit into how this was intended to go down. This experience taught me a new way of praying for others, leaving *what I feel should be done* out of the equation!

### FINDING NEW SPACE

Bernie and I, looking for a new home, had been taking rides in any direction there was a new development being built. I've always known I would not be spending my senior years in Rutherford, NJ. We had recently lost both of our mothers, and on this particular weekend in 1999, we headed to Central Jersey to check out a development we heard about called *Winding Ways*. As we neared the place, we passed a Catholic church called Saint Aloysius.

Hmmmm, immediately I said silently to myself, "Hi Ei! (my mother-in-law). Say, Ei, if this is the right place for us, give us several signs; this church being the first. Bernie's mother, Eileen had graduated from St. Aloysius (Al-o-ish-us), in Jersey City, NJ. We drove for another mile; and lo and behold, we make a left turn onto South Cook's Bridge Road! "Oh Lord, Cook was Eileen's maiden name!"

We drove into the community and checked out the new homes, which were great. As we were leaving, Bernie said, "Let's ride around this community to see what it's like." While cruising around, I saw someone walking up the road a bit and said, "Hey Bernie, that's your cousin Ned." Bernie said, "Get the hell outa' here!" I finished by saying, "Better take a second look!" It was Ned who just happened to be the nephew of Eileen Cook Kahrar!

Ned invited us into his new home and told us all about their community. In passing, he mentioned that across the street they had plans to build a new community called Westlake, only this community would have a golf course. Need I say more? We moved in one and one-half years later and have never stopped feeling this was a very wise move for us. How could we lose, with three distinct signs from someone we knew loved us dearly?

NOTES:

NOTES:

# CHAPER IV

## 2000

### A CHILD IS COMING

At the end of 1999, Bernie and I sold our home of twenty-eight years and moved into an adult community in central New Jersey. In the summer of 2001, our breakfast over, I was checking some items I had listed on E-bay. Very relaxed, leaning on my hand, I glanced out my office door into the hallway; walking toward me was a vision of a toddler, with very curly white hair, wearing only a Pamper. Can't tell if it's a little boy or little girl, but I instinctively put my hand over my heart and whispered to this child, "Ooooh, you are sooo cute!"

Next, I filled with emotion and tears ran down my cheeks. I realized that in this vision, a grandchild was coming! I could see right through the child, instinctively knowing that it was another sacred hologram! I ran through the house to find Bernie who, startled at seeing me crying, asked what's going on. I told him, "Bernie, I don't know who, I don't know when, but a grandchild is coming and it will have white hair and a mass of curls!

What must this husband of mine think of me? Oh well, it doesn't really matter, does it? I told Bernie it was a hologram, just like the ones we saw at Disney World. Sure enough, later that fall our Bryan and Licette informed us that a child was coming in May of 2002. To compound the situation, Jocelynn and Rob told us in March that they were expecting in November of 2002. Gee, they overlap, so did I see the first or the second grandchild? I must be patient because; in our family it takes a full two years before the babies have any hair. I needed to wait patiently until they were toddlers to get my answer.

One day an upset, pregnant Licette called me to say a good friend had lost her baby and what would she do if she lost hers? I was able to comfort her because I had seen the hologram of a baby toddling towards me. Our little Tyler was born in May 2002 to Bryan and Licette, and when he was around two years old, his hair was straight but oh, so white! Our little granddaughter, Sydney was born in November of 2002, and as a two year old had light blonde hair, but hers was a solid mass of curls! I then realized that this hologram or vision that I saw was a composite of the both of them. Amazing!

## MY POWER ANIMAL

I met a new friend named Lonnie in our community, who is a *biofeedback* instructor, and she invited me to join her for meditation and drumming sessions with a friend of hers who was a Shaman. When she asked I quickly responded, "You bet!" Before we even started this bi-weekly class, I prayed before going to sleep, and asked God to show me my power animal. Surely it would be an eagle, owl, or bear! As you can see there is still nothing wrong with my ego. (Incidentally, ego means *"Easing God Out!"*— E. Joyce 2/12/81)

74

As I began waking up the next morning, while my eyes were still closed, I rolled over on my side and in my mind's eye, sitting on its haunches staring back at me, was a gray goat! "Oh Lord, not a goat! Maybe you meant a regal ram, or most certainly a white mountain goat, Lord?!" By now I have learned this attitude of mine is not such a good one, so, however dutifully, I said a short, "Thank-you God, for goat." As the days passed, I continued to thank God for goat, and blessed all goats that inhabited our planet as I tried to persuade my love and respect for "goat" to grow.

One Sunday, a couple of weeks later, Bernie was out golfing and in the afternoon. I sat down, turned on the TV; and as I passed *Animal Planet* an hour program was beginning on, of all things, "Goats!"

I no longer question these instances of *sacred synchronicity*, as I knew it was meant for me to watch this program. I ran for a pad of paper to make sure I was ready to write down all the "positive and negative" attributes of goat. Top of the list: a goat is stubborn, it's nothing for them to give you a head butt for no apparent reason, and oh Lord, they eat anything in sight! I sat there quite perplexed because the more I learned about Goat, the more I saw the resemblance!

On the positive side, they are steadfast, nurturing, loyal, care very much about their kids. They also are adventurous and can climb anything. It is my honor to honor all parts of myself that are most definitely like Goat!

## SEVEN WORDS THAT CHANGED MY LIFE

Sleep is not going to happen and I must write because this incident is repeatedly rolling around my mind. How can I set the stage for this one? I promise I'll keep it as simple as possible. My parents were intense. I have often said, "Living with our mother was like living with mother Mary, and our Dad was the polar opposite." Growing up, the saving grace for us was Dad loved his job as a railroad engineer, worked long, grueling hours, therefore his time home with us was short. Dad loved us, but there are few who would ever disagree we were second in line behind his beloved trains. Because of this my mother, sister, and I became a "girls club," more often than not leaving Dad as "odd man out."

When mother became ill, she would tell my sister, Bonnie and me, "There is something wrong with you father's head." Mother was weak and needed so much care that my sister and I were both happy Dad could wash and dress himself. She also asked us to, "Care for your father." We both heard her say this, but we each had a different take on how this would need to be accomplished. After mother passed, within several months, T.I.A.'s, and seizures hit my father, and it became all too apparent our Dad was much worse than we suspected. Bonnie took him in. I need to say here, this would not have been an option as far as I was concerned; I would have given money to make sure he was well cared for, because Dad more than filled a room for me. There seemed to always be blocks between Dad and I whenever we tried to get close.

Over time, saying that Dad's strong will and erratic personality took its toll on Bonnie and her marriage, would be an understatement. In Dad's defense, he couldn't help it and was doing erratic "head things" although this certainly didn't make it any easier to be around him. The day came when it was quite apparent my sister needed me to kick in to help with Dad's care. My concern and deep love for her was the only reason I said, "Yes." The schedule my sister came up with was she would have Dad for two months, we would take him for one month, then he would return to her and the cycle would repeat.

Dad was born and raised in Maryland, and loved my younger sister so he was more content in his home state at her home than he was at mine in NJ. Whenever he was in New Jersey, I took him to the ocean daily, when the weather was good, and attended baseball games. Bernie took us around to see all the sights of the metropolitan area, always making sure to take pictures for an album so Dad would remember all we did together while he was in New Jersey.

I don't know if the above was simple enough for you, but I did my best to condense a complicated situation. Getting to the point, it is countdown time, and Dad will be coming up in another month for one month. I began to constantly pray and talk to God. I want things to go smoothly for Dad, my husband, and me while he was here. During the month leading up to his visit, my prayer was, "Dear God, please let me unconditionally love this difficult man." Over and over I prayed this simple prayer and now with Dad's visit looming, I added, "God, I promise you there will be no tension or arguing this time; whatever Dad says I'll agree with, just please help me unconditionally love this difficult man."

Dad arrived. He loved Court TV, and I fed him his favorite foods and fruits and was on call for whatever he needed. The nights were extremely unsettling because Dad's personality was always volatile, and now he had become a "sundowner." This meant he did really, absurd, nutty things when the sun went down; with no medical explanations. All in all, though this visit really was going along well because I agreed with everything Dad said and did.

When Dad was absorbed in TV, and was comfy, fed and watered, I attempted to go into my office for a few minutes alone. Pretty soon, Dad searched for me, found me at my desk, and plopped down in the loveseat behind me.

This time I was paying bills but when Dad came in, I switched to a game of solitaire - it's not always important I "be there" when Dad's mind goes from one thing to another. We started talking about different things, the beach, Maryland, and when he brought my sister's name up I said, "Bonnie is such a good person." Dad said, "She sure is," and then he said, "You know, I loved your sister more."

I spun around on my office chair and put my hands on his knees saying, "Oh Dad, I am so glad you said that. First of all, I want you to know that I always felt cared for...home, food, clothes, doctors, dentists and vacations. I think what your saying is not that you loved Bonnie more, but that you got along better with Bonnie than me." Hearing this, he says, "Well, that's true." I continued with, "Isn't it a good thing now that I'm grown up and we can get along?" He agreed. I turned around to face my desk, my head spinning.

His moment of lucidity faded quickly, and Dad's mind trailed off as he said, "The next time you come to Maryland, we'll go down to mom's crypt, open her up and see how she's fairing?" I responded, "Sure, Dad!" After all, I am agreeing with everything he says, but my head is still spinning! His words didn't hurt me they explained all the craziness from my youth. While Dad rambled on, I humbly thanked God for this miracle that set me free.

After that, whenever Dad realized I was not within his range, he would come looking for me and when he saw me he would tilt his head back, throw his arms out and sing an old song, *"I love you; I love you, more than words can say."* I would melt into those hugs, absorbing all the heartfelt love coming to me from my Dad, and amazingly all those old hurtful memories forever faded away.

This was no minor miracle, if there is such a thing! Yep, those seven little words melted every resentful, angry memory and changed the energy between Dad and me. My heart is deeply grateful and I considered this a major turning point in my life.

## DAD ENTERS A NURSING HOME

Shortly after this awareness, Dad took a turn for the worse and was rushed to the hospital. Then he went from the hospital into a nursing home. My sister, Bonnie, ever faithful in her care of Dad; transferred her devoted care from her home to her many visits to Dad in the V.A. Nursing Home. She continued doing Dad's laundry, taking him special meals and treats. I drove down every couple of weeks to bring him the favorite meals I knew he liked as well as to keep his hair trimmed. He had been in the V.A. home for a month when Bernie and I, our pregnant daughter, Jocelynn, my sister Bonnie, and her husband Earl, gathered to visit Dad. All the family members fussed over him and we laughed our way through the afternoon. When visiting hours ended, we began to gather all our things.

There is a half-gate the nurses open to let visitors in and lock after they leave. Dad remained inside the protected area. All of us were talking and laughing when I casually turned to look back, and saw Dad in an absolute panic, walking in circles. My eyes filled with tears because for years I held so much anger and resentment towards him. I was angry because of how he talked and occasionally treated our Mother. Of course, I loved my father, but this one incident brought home to me the fact I had never had compassion in my heart for him until I saw the fear in his eyes. My heart broke to see him so scared and afraid.

I walked back to the gate and called him over. He walked towards me and I said, "Dad, look me in the eyes! You have to stay here until they correct your level of medicines, but I want you to know, Bonnie and I know

79

where you are and we will always be able to get to you!" Then I told him I loved him. Dad calmed down and we left. After that incident, the family visited him as often as possible.

The next summer, Bonnie and Earl decided to go on a cruise. I needed to go down for two weekends to check on Dad, do his laundry, and visit. My nephew David, joined me the first weekend and then my sons, Bryan and James made the second trip with me to see him on what turned out to be the next to the last time I would ever see my father. Bernie and I went to Virginia for three days for his job and on the way home we stopped by the V.A. Nursing Home to see Dad but he was not there! He had taken ill and had been transferred to John Hopkins in Baltimore, MD. I looked at Bernie and said, "It would break my heart if I don't see him again." We turned the car around and headed south to Baltimore.

Dad was in a private room. The nurse at the desk told us that morning a chaplain stopped by and asked him if he had any family. Dad's words were, "Yes, they know where I am and they are coming." These words of his still bring me deep comfort, as I know I got through to him that day months before, as we were leaving. For me, the worst thing would have been if Dad felt he was alone and thought we weren't able to get to him.

When we arrived at his bedside, Dad was concerned about *the door behind the closed curtain.* Bernie finally got on a chair and moved the curtain to show Dad it was only a window, not a door. Dad said, "Oh, okay" We had to reassure him about this "door" several times and the next day, when he passed away after a dive in blood pressure, I realized that the door he had been so concerned about turned out to be his *doorway for crossing over.*

## MARCO, THE COCKATEIL

I have always loved animals, but since I am allergic, we couldn't bring them into the house. The brilliant idea came to me that we should have some sort of pet when the kids were young and I thought birds would be a good idea. Bernie knew someone who had a bird store, so we all piled into the car. Parrots were everywhere on life-sized wooden fences, but I couldn't have that, so we ended up with two cockatiels that the owner said were friends. He put them in a box and we brought them home with us. Bernie said that these two were such good friends that they were mating the whole trip home! Anyway, we bought the nesting box and over the next several years ended up with about twelve, hand-raised little feathered friends. They quickly outgrew the cage and Bernie constructed a larger pen. I think we had some happy birds for a long time. One side of the family room eventually became the bird room. One little fella was so adventurous, the kids named him Marco (for Marco Polo), and one day, unfortunately, he flew into a blowfish that was part of my nautical decoration. He spent some time in the hospital cage but ever after, he walked with a limp. Eventually, as time passed, we gave them away, all except one, Marco.

The kids went away to college and when we relocated to Central Jersey we brought Marco with us. The door was always open to his cage and he enjoyed his home in our new family room. Time has a way of passing when you aren't looking but one day I noticed his feathers weren't shiny anymore so, the spring of his twenty-third year I took him to the vet who sent us home to enjoy the two or three months we had left with this loving member of our family.

We heaped love on this kind, enjoyable bird; gave him his favorite string beans, seeds, extra vitamins and every month extra we had with him, I considered a blessing. Instead of two-three, we had six months more! He eventually went blind and we had thick blankets on the table, under his cage, as well as around the floor so, when he walked off the edge, he wouldn't land on anything hard.

Bernie would have no part with putting Marco down, so my prayer was, *"Dear God, if it has to be done, I will do it, but only if I see his cage is not his safe haven anymore. Amen."* We would shut his door if we were going out because we didn't want him to hurt himself.

One day, I was at the kitchen sink, doing dishes and watching Marco. He worked his way over to get a drink and fell into his drinking water. If I hadn't been there, it would have been over because Marco was too weak to save himself! Oh my God! His cage was no longer his safe haven! I called the vet, who graciously let me bring him in at the end of the day.

In the Vet's office, I was holding Marco in my hands, and although his eyes were closed, he was still grooming my nails. We watched him with love and sadness, and the Vet told me that Marco was an awesome bird. I gently placed him in the soft cloth she was holding; Marco fluffed up, lowered his head, and within five minutes he was gone.

Bernie was relieved that it was over before he came home from his business trip, and he lovingly built the box and planned the burial. Marco had been one of the eggs from our first brood.

One year later, I was in the family room reading in the wee hours because when Bernie snores, one of us has to leave the bed. I was reading a book when something sparked a memory of Marco. As I put the book down, I thought, "Marco, it's been a year and we have never heard from you." Now, I don't know why I had that thought.

After my shower the next morning, I was drying my hair with the bathroom door shut, when I thought I heard a bird in our family room. I turned off the hairdryer, opened the door and listened; "Geeze, I must be hearing things, there is no bird here."

After breakfast, Bernie and I were sitting at the table talking. I was going through the weekly advertisements so I could throw them away, when I turned a page and there was a Franklin Mint advertisement picturing a gray cockatiel with orange and yellow cheeks.

Silently, it came together and I realized Marco heard me in the middle of the night. It was his call I heard as I was drying my hair! There he sat so proudly on a branch in the advertisement looking at me! I started to cry; Bernie noticed my tears, and asked, "Is it something I did?" I told him no, then told him my story. He listened and very pragmatically asked, "Does this mean we have to buy it?" Today, porcelain Marco sits proudly on top of our china cabinet surrounded by flowers, overseeing all that goes on just like he loved to do.

## THE ANSWER

This adventure is the answer to a twenty-year quest. How often have I thought of that dream I had in the late 1980's (see: *A Dream Like No Other* and *My Guru —Pg. 31*) and it has always left me wondering. We have lived in our community for eight years and four years earlier I met and became friends with Ulli and her husband Frank. Ulli may very well be one of the deepest seekers of Spiritual knowledge I have met in this lifetime.

The Christmas before she and Frank moved back to Austria, she invited her good friend Ingebourg, to come to the United States. I spent several afternoons in their company and on the last afternoon, I asked Ingebourg exactly what she was is interested in and she told me she "works with the Masters." Upon hearing this, I experienced a deep longing. My prayer becomes, *"Lord, I feel I am ready to work with Master Energies. If I am not, make me ready or use me as I am. In all things that I ask, your will, not mine be done. Amen."* I'm not a haunt in this request, but I mention it in my dialogue whenever it pops into my head. I belong to a women's group that meets every Friday. This meeting is written in stone, and we all enjoy our "search for deeper meaning" group.

One day, we met at Liz's home and at the end of the afternoon, she told us to pick from a selection of Spiritual books on her coffee table. The routine was; close your eyes, quiet yourself, and ask about something you needed to know. When ready, we were to randomly open the book we chose, pick a spot on the page, then open our eyes, and read our answer.

This is something like Bible-Bingo and I have used this method every once in a while to gain a little insight. This day, I chose a small book, *The Alchemist* by Paul Coelho, quieted myself and mentally said, "It's the same old question Lord, when will I be ready to work with the Master Energies?"

With eyes closed, I opened the book, picked a page and slid my finger down to what was the third line. I opened my eyes to read. The line spoke about a young boy being guided into the tent; an opulent tent with carpet thicker than any he had ever seen, with ten gold chandeliers hanging. There were eight chieftains seated and one moved forward to greet him and invite him in. At this point, I looked up at Liz, and giggled out loud, because I *knew* my prayer was about to be answered! I was excited to see how the rest of this inner realization would unfold.

The next day Bernie attended a family communion without me because our niece had cats and I was recovering from a bout of bronchitis. I was at my computer, paying bills and listening to a radio program. The woman being interviewed (Rosemary Ellen Guiley) spoke about 'dreaming' on a Soul level. She said, "One can experience an energy transfer called *Shaktipat*. I quickly paused the interview and Googled Shaktipat." Google corrected my spelling and many, many websites popped up. A lot of them mentioned this *Mahavatar Babaji*, the Immortal Himalayan Yogi. They spoke about this *blessing* of an energy transfer that is given to devotees that are pure of heart.

Eventually, I opened one website that had a painting of Babaji, and as soon as my eyes fell upon this face I began a slow-leak cry that lasted for hours because this was the woman in my dream from twenty years before! Only this Babaji that gave this Shaktipat wasn't a woman; Babaji happened to be androgynous.

It's too big to mention to Bernie and that night we went out with friends. I returned home to find my former 'guru,' Elizabeth Joyce, had emailed me out of the blue about a psychic fair she'd be working at in Summerville, NJ. How rare is this? We only touched base at Christmas. Yep, sacred synchronicity, for sure! I emailed her back and said I'd received the answer to a twenty-year mystery. I had a dream about White Light and always wondered what it was, what it meant, and why I had the dream?

Elizabeth quickly answered saying, "This blessing is one people wait years and lifetimes for. It is a true blessing from God. It's often called The Holy Spirit, the Western terminology, or Shaktipat, the Eastern terminology. I'll make it simple. It's a kiss from God, and happens in sleep when you are receiving a Divine Blessing."

I longed to work with the Master Energies, and it seemed this Divine, healing energy had been flowing through me for twenty years. Do Avatars have a sense of humor, or do they just love to see us floundering about? The meaning of the word Avatar is *a multi-dimensional being that has finished all the cycles of aIn-soph sephirot and has come to Earth to aid other beings and life forms with their Soul Ascension.*

I read a lot of websites and this is what I found: Mahavitar Babaji gives a Spiritual blessing only attained after the highest level of God Realization, experienced by those of many faiths who develop devotion combined with purity. It is said Babaji enlightened the Christ and is also called the "Deathless Master."

It seems spiritual awakening, or Shaktipat, lies at the heart of the mystical journey. Honestly, all I did was start an inner dialogue with God back in the 1980's, and each voice I heard changed my life for the better. Is it possible to be humbled any more than I am? YEEEEESSSSS!

## GOD REALIZATION

I found this written in *The Art of Spiritual Healing*, Joel Goldsmith, 1992, years ago and it struck a chord with me. I have always kept copies around so I could re-read it occasionally.

> *Unless you go to God for but one purpose—for God and God alone—you are acknowledging two powers; good and evil. You expect God the big, good power, to do something to the nasty little evil power. Neither rest— nor peace will ever come, as you are waiting for a great big God to fix something you perceive to be incorrect or in error. Peace will come only when you can sit quietly in realization. (Think about this prayer: "Thank you Father, all I expect of your word is that it will burst the bubble,*

*pierce the veil, because harmony already is. I would not be here waiting to hear Your Voice if I believed there were disharmony and discord.") Want God only for the purpose of God-realization. What God does to you or to your affairs is an entirely different matter. The minute you try to direct God to bring you companionship, a home, occupation, talent, or a certain outcome —then God becomes the means to an end. When you think about it; it is almost blasphemous - this idea of using God - and yet the commonly accepted concept of prayer is that God will do something for you, or that by your words God can be influenced in the right direction. This is NOT prayer, and is why most prayer is not effective. The only effective prayer is the attainment of God realization.*

My prayer now is one of acceptance—*"Thy will be done."*

NOTES:

# CHAPTER V

## 2010

### IT IS HIS HONOR TO DO THIS

Feeling mentally tired, I was laying my head down on the pillow, when I realized I was barnstorming the ethers with the same questions when a voice suddenly interrupted me saying, *IT IS HIS HONOR TO DO THIS!* Like lightening I said to myself, "It is HIS honor to do THIS? It's HIS honor to do WHAT? What does THIS mean? It's WHOSE honor, Jesus'? Does this mean there is truth to what religion says? Does this mean I have misunderstood? I am no longer so sure of myself! If it is "His Honor," this, to me, means HE CHOSE to do THIS!!

After I had the experience, I got right back up and went to the computer. I wrote the following email to Bill Donohue at *HiddenMeanings.com*. I have followed this man since the early 1990's and he connects Quantum Physics with ancient texts, explaining them so anyone can understand.

"Dear Bill: from my mid-thirties on, it has been my path to get direct messages from this level that you are so beautifully

digging apart and scientifically explaining. You have profoundly helped me to make sense of the things that have happened to me."

(Following is my story along with his answer to my experience. Bill Donohue's answers are in bold, italicized letters.)

I have questioned religions and the sanity of them for the longest time now, and am convinced they are one of the root causes of war, creating way too much tension around the world. Personally, I am at the point where I don't even want to celebrate Christmas, forget any other "holy" day!

*IT IS SUCH A TRAGEDY OF LIFE, THAT THE ONES WHO ALIGN THEMSELVES WITH THE BEAUTIFUL PACIFISM OF JESUS, AT THE SAME TIME PROMOTE FEAR, SUSPICIONS, AND DOWNRIGHT VIOLENCE AMONG PEOPLE, ESPECIALLY THOSE WHO ARE MEMBERS OF THEIR PARTICULAR GROUP.*

I keep sending my questions out to God, Spirit, and the Universe. Is all this BS? Edgar Cayce, in his book, *Many Mansions,* stated a quote; *In my house are many mansions.* Perhaps that's where our focus should be.

*FOCUS ON THE TRUE NATURE OF THE LIGHT/ PHOTON, WHICH SACRIFICES ITS OWN PROPERTIES TO MAKE US ONE WITH A HIGHER PROPERTY. IN THAT TRUTH LIES THE MEANING OF THE ONE LIGHT, WHO MUST BE SACRIFICED TO MAKE US ONE WITH THE HIGHER LIGHT. IT IS A WONDERFUL THING THAT TAKES PLACE IN GOLGOTHA—WHICH MEANS SKULL. RIGHT THERE IT ALL TAKES PLACE.*

I do, occasionally have 'Jesus' guilt from my youth thanks to my sweet Mama's upbringing and I have been praying; asking and re-asking where is the Truth hidden in all this?

*THE TRUTH IN ALL OF THIS IS FLOWING TO ME THROUGH YOUR WORDS RIGHT NOW. THE TRUTH IN ALL OF THIS IS WITHIN YOU. AS THE ORACLE OF DELPHI SAID, "TO THINE OWN SELF, BE TRUE." TRUST OF THE OPINIONS OF ANOTHER IS MEANINGLESS. ONLY WHEN YOU ARE PART OF THE LHT MOVEMENT WITHIN WILL YOU EXPERIENCE TRUTH. YOU OBVIOUSLY HAVE.*

Recently I have been reading a wonderful book, *Sage-ing While Age-ing by* Shirley McLain who shares her Spiritual adventures with the world. I especially enjoyed the last several chapters of her views on religion.

Well, on this night in June, I couldn't sleep because my husband was snoring loudly, so I got up around two A.M., went into my lounge chair in our family room to finish reading Shirley McLain's book. After about an hour of reading, I closed the book because I was sleepy. I woke up about four A.M., thinking to myself, "Gee, I don't hear snoring anymore; maybe I can go back to bed." I gingerly got up from my lounge chair and rather unsteadily made my way back into bed. I was sitting on the edge of the bed thinking how I enjoyed Shirley's information on religion, God and Jesus, realizing that many of our Christian belief views have changed since I was a girl.

*THINK OF JESUS AS THE PUREST PHOTON WITHIN THE DYNAMIC ETHER THAT PENETRATES THE VERY BEING OF ALL LIFE. THINK OF THAT PHOTON RESURRECTING WITHIN EACH BEING THE ABSOLUTE PEACE AND COMMUNION OF NATURE FREE FROM THE HANDS OF THE MERCHANT ONES.*

As I laid my head down on the pillow, I realized I was once again barnstorming the ethers with the same questions. This is when the experience occurred. Like lightening a voice interrupted me to say: *IT IS HIS HONOR TO DO THIS.*

*INDEED IT IS HIS HONOR TO ORIGINATE THE THOUGHTS AND TRUTHS THAT ARE FLOWING FROM YOU NOW. IT IS HIS HONOR TO FIND YOU FILLED WITH THE UNDERSTANDING OF YOUR INNER SELF AND YOUR REJECTION OF THE DOCTRINES OF FEAR AND VIOLENCE THAT HAVE BEEN ORDAINED FROM CHURCH TO CHURCH, TEMPLE TO TEMPLE, AND MOSQUE TO MOSQUE. IT IS HIS HONOR THAT YOU ARE FOLLOWING HIS PATH TO A HIGHER LIGHT THAT MAY FLOURISH IN THIS CREATION.*

Of course, now my mind is wide awake and one thing is apparent, I have heard another voice, it will make me think long and hard, and I know from personal experience my life and the way I live is changing once again.

*THERE IS NOTHING SO PERMANENT AS CHANGE.*

Thank you Bill Donahue, for your Divine wisdom.


## YOU KNOW LORD, YOU'RE RIGHT!

Ahhh, summer's almost over! This morning in late August, Bernie and I were making a run up to North Jersey to give our son a cast iron dutch oven. I was out of the shower, drying my hair and thinking to myself, "Oh goody, today we get to see all the grandkids, and I lovingly thought of each one— Tyler, Lindsay, Sydney, Robby, Mia, and Nolan and maybe our Samantha who was away at school!"

A voice interrupted my thoughts saying, "Bryan and Licette are hippies." I answered it quite naturally, "... you know, Lord, you're right, they really are! Some of their friends even dress like hippies. They're a throwback to the 60's! It's like they're in a time-warp and they've missed their time by fifty years!"

I happily finished styling my hair and after we finished breakfast, we were on our way. We stopped by Bryan and Licette's home first, sometimes it is the other way around and we visit them last before our one hundred mile run home. Bryan said he wanted to talk with us and he told us his family wanted to sell their home, buy a u-drive'em trailer and hit the road for up to ten years.

Licette joined us at the kitchen table. I was not as shocked as Bernie. The Divine voice I heard that morning prepared me and, instead of fear, I more easily slipped into, "This will be a great adventure," mode. I am ever thankful for the voices I hear.

## I STAND AMAZED

Bernie and I were going up to North Jersey so he could give a talk about community service to six-year-old Mia's first grade class. All went very smoothly and afterwards we went to James and Madelyn's home. James and his friend Tim arrived after work and everyone was talking and having a good time. Bernie went inside and I remained in the back yard with Tim. Our conversation began about James. Tim told me that James is wonderful, that no matter what they talk about, James can add something uplifting to it. He told me that, "James gets it!"

We felt a certain synchronicity and Tim opened up and told me that he belonged to a group of thousands of people. I asked him if it was a religion or a group; he hemmed and hawed just a little before telling me that,

"Without going into it all," he had a substance abuse problem. I told him I understood and that, "food was still my drug of choice." I'm not sure if we mentioned AA at this point, but he questioned me again about how James just seems to "know" and that he adds something positive to whatever they talk about.

I opened up to Tim and told him that my mother was born into a family whose father had been a binge drinker. When mother married Dad, alcohol wasn't even allowed in our home. She considered alcohol really bad, and mother considered the verbal abuse she received from Dad a step up! (She told me once she had always been grateful that Dad never hit her!). It was a different age for her - they didn't have the tools needed, so she wasn't able to change things; therefore, my sister and I had to deal with our own obsessions.

My saving grace was I married Bernie and moved to New Jersey. When we had problems I was encouraged to go for personal and marriage counseling, and life really changed for me when I began reading Norman Vincent Peale's book *The Power of Positive Thinking*. Somewhere in our conversation, Tim asked me if I had ever gone to AL-A-NON. I told him no, but I had a neighbor who gave me a book called, *One Day at a Time*, and after that I made sure I bought one for the next four or five years. Every day, before work, I read and reflected on the daily reading. As I took the twelve steps to heart, I began to enlarge my concepts of what God is; apologized for my offenses, etc., etc.

All of a sudden, Tim's arms rose up and he was looking toward the heavens! "I understand where James gets it, I finally understand! I get it! It was you, you lived it!" I was dumbfounded and could only shake my head *yes*, as I realized the vital part this wonderful organization had played in my family. I have never taken the credit and have always said prayer is what helped our children make their choices not to depend on smoking, drinking, or doing drugs to help them cope with life's problems.

I stood there amazed and extremely humbled as Tim sparked my memory. Truly, it hit me for the first time the huge impact Alcoholics Anonymous had played in our lives! My gratitude overflowed.

## THIS 'SPLAINS' EVERYTHING!

I handed out some copies of this book to my family and friends and they have encouraged me with their comments, phone calls and feedback. That's the way this day started out. I was feeling inspired, as if my words had touched a heart.

Every so often, something happens to trigger a louder than normal argument between my husband and myself. Honestly, it started off so innocently when we decided to go to the ocean and walk the boardwalk.

On the ride over, I was enthusiastically talking to Bernie about the book that has been in the works for twelve years, when I glanced over and saw that he had curled his upper lip and made a "shoosh" sound. Like I said, occasionally an old monster will raise its head. I was so hurt by his silent put-down and am not proud to say I went off on him— *pretty* badly! Bernie told me I didn't have good self-esteem.

Obviously, my very modest, conventional husband is not at all confident how my God-experience will be accepted. Bernie had two illustrious careers; honored by many countless awards for not only his bravery but for his many years of great detective and investigative work. We'd have no problem in wallpapering a good-sized wall!

Since our therapy and marriage counseling so long ago, my self-esteem is not an issue. Don't really care who you are, I call 'em when they happen; choosing not to keep my feelings in to stew on for months or years. Besides, working away from low self-esteem had been a huge part of my journey!

Back to the present: This boardwalk was two feet higher than the road and Bernie jumped up. I put two quarters in the meter which only gave us thirty minutes, so I went around the car, got another quarter, put it in the meter; we now had forty-five minutes. I looked up and asked, "Is that long enough?" As I was gazing into Bernie's eyes, this *voice* blasted,

*"He saves lives! You save souls!"*

This one voice gave me the confirmation *On Common Ground* was never just my story, but needed to be shared. This voice was major! Each voice caused me to change my life!

God has more than shown me I am cared for and that I have never walked my path alone.

*Without a sound the battle's done*
*The war is won, and Peace begins.*

—Johnathan Trueblood

NOTES:

NOTES:

# SHARON'S RECOMMENDED BOOK LIST
## The * means highly recommended – read this one first!

*You Own The Power*                    – Rosemary Altea

*Spontaneous Healing*              – Gregg Braden

*Ageless Body – Timeless Mind*   – Dr. Deepak Chopra

*How To Know God*               – Dr. Deepak Chopra

*The Immortal*                   – J.J. Dewey

*Initiation*                      – Elizabeth Haich

*Seeding and Nurturing the Garden of Your Soul*

                          —Elizabeth Joyce

*The Power of Force*           –   David Hawkins

*You Can Heal Your Life*        – Louise Hay

*The Worlds Greatest Psychics*   – Francine Hornberger

*The Remnant*                 – Mary La Croix

*Dying To Be Me*             — Anita Moorjani

*The Pathwork of Self-Transformation*  – Eva Pierrakos

# SHARON'S RECOMMENDED BOOK LIST

## *(Continued)*

*The Timeless Path*     –     Swami Ramakrishananda Puri

*The Third Eye*     – T. Lobsang Rampa

*Love, Medicine & Miracles*     – Dr. Bernie E. Siegel

*The Unthered Soul*     – Michael A. Singer

*Man's Etenal Quest*     – Parmahansa Yogananda

*The Autobiography of A Yogi*

    – Parmahansa Yogananda

(The books referred to throughout this book are also included as a part of this list.)

# ABOUT THE AUTHOR

## SHARON KAHRAR

**SHARON KAHRAR** was born, raised, and educated in Maryland. She married Bernie Kahrar, and moved to Bergen County, New Jersey. Together they raised three children and are now enjoying their seven grandchildren. Both are retired now, but Sharon loved her secretarial career. Sharon became an avid reader, lover of the arts, enjoys sculpturing, writing and traveling. However, she has found that her greatest adventure is walking daily with Spirit, which is the focus of *On Common Ground*. Her daily journaling over the years have brought us the wise Spiritual knowledge contained within these pages.

**Website:** http://sharonkahrar24.net

On Common Ground

www.ingramcontent.com/pod-product-compliance
Lightning Source LLC
Chambersburg PA
CBHW071007040426
42443CB00007B/701